D1527331

BEYOND BLACK and WHITE

~

Love, Race, and Jazz in the '60s

Gerard Wiggins

Printed in the United States of America

ISBN 979-8-86191-921-0

Design and Layout: Jeff DiPerna
Cover Painting: Gerard Wiggins

FOR BOBBY

CONTENTS

PART THREE: SODEN STREET

PROLOGUE

The Wiggins family can trace its lineage back to the Massachusetts Bay Colony. In 1639, Thomas Wiggin (my father and uncle added the "s") settled in what would become Stratham, New Hampshire, and became governor of the surrounding area. Several generations later, members of the Wiggin family had settled in Vermont.

In 1928, at the age of 14, my father, Dick, left his Vermont home with his twin brother, Bob, to escape the wrath of their stepmother. In Tilton, New Hampshire, they worked for a great uncle on his cattle farm but found pumping gas at a filling station more to their liking.

In 1938, my father married Ruth, a college-educated woman from the Midwest. He was the first in the family to marry someone from outside New England. Hoping to avoid active combat during WWII, my mother and father (with his brother in tow) moved to San Diego to work in an aircraft factory.

Nevertheless, my Uncle Bob served in the South Pacific. After the war, the three returned to New Hampshire to start an antiques business.

In the 1950s, life in rural New Hampshire was tough, especially for a dealer who depended on selling antiques to well-heeled summer residents. Before the interstate, few found their way to Sanbornton to buy antiques during the cold winter. Our family struggled. More than once, our phone service was cut, and the town threatened to sell our house for back taxes. But my older brother and I were never aware of the full extent of our poverty.

In grade school, I struggled to keep up academically, unaware of having dyslexia. Fortunately my parents never showed disappointment in their son, who lagged behind. Their constant love and support enabled me to plow through the most painful years in high school.

My father and uncle were accomplished tennis players and patiently tried to interest me in the sport, but without success. Summer ball games behind the grade school, where fathers and sons teamed up, were as enjoyable for me as going to the dentist. Out of step with my environment, I wondered if I could find anything to identify with. The first time I heard Miles Davis' trumpet, I felt as if I'd sighted land after being lost at sea. Thus began a passion that would carry me through the turmoil of adolescence and beyond.

After I moved to Boston and childhood ways were left behind, a door opened into the fascinating world of jazz and a society which had been unknown to me, although it had existed in plain sight. More surprisingly, I found love where I never expected. The impact of these few years in Boston laid the foundation for the rest of my life.

PART ONE

EARLY DAYS

CHAPTER 1

RUNNING DOWN THE *JAZZ TRACK*

My window seat looked out on the turboprop engine of the Icelandic aircraft. While all other transatlantic airline companies had gone jet-propelled, Icelandic, the cheapest and safest, still used prop planes. When the engines cranked up, a cloud of black smoke spewed out of the rear, accompanied by a vibration so violent I thought the fillings in my teeth would drop out. *Maybe this is normal*, I guessed. Since this was my maiden voyage, I had nothing to compare it with. No one else seemed overly concerned, so I sat back and did my best to relax.

Once airborne, the vibrating diminished enough for a pretty stewardess to serve soft drinks. Watching the coast of Maine in miniature, my agitated mind started obsessing over landing in Luxembourg without speaking French. Growing more frantic, I rebuked myself, *I must have been clean out of my mind to leave my friends, Arthur, Dos, Chops, and Steve. And Bobby?* Now wasn't the time to reanalyze all he had put us through, especially me. Would I ever have such a hip scene as we had on Anderson Street, with the constant flow of people and continual jazz playing? Would there be a jazz club showcasing great musicians, the way Boston's Jazz Workshop did, in London or Paris?

As the landscape out my window diminished, so did my conviction. I wondered how I could have talked myself into the belief that traveling around Europe alone was a bright idea. The recent traumas that had defined 1968 contributed to my decision to leave town, but there was more to it than social upheaval. *What was the trajectory that landed me in this seat?* I asked myself.

The daylight had faded and my fellow passengers had dozed off. With nothing else to do, I put my life on rewind to find a starting point. Best as I could see, it began with the beguiling sound of jazz.

Like most young children, the world fascinated me. Finding seasonal ponds in the woods with frogs' eggs hatching into tadpoles, peepers keeping me awake in the spring, watching a tiger butterfly feeding on nectar—all of it captured my attention. Then, when I was ten, an unexpected event opened the way to my interior world.

The pursuits that would determine the direction of my life, jazz being only one of them, came through my older brother David. When he received Miles Davis' *Jazz Track* from the Columbia Record Club, I tried to follow him and his friend to hear the new LP. At the threshold, they said, "Not today, kid; you're too young for jazz." Those words hung in the air as the door closed. *I'll show 'em*, I thought. Sitting on the floor outside the door, I waited. Then the haunting sound of a trumpet drifted out into the hallway and straight to my heart. After a few sparse notes from the bass and piano, the trumpet returned with the most wistful sound I'd ever heard. I dared not move, afraid of missing something. The depth of feeling this music evoked was far beyond my grasp. But the way it was expressed, I found curiously easy to understand. Instinctively, I knew the answer to many future questions would be found between and through the notes.

In short order, Miles' *Porgy and Bess* and *Sketches of Spain* arrived via the record club. By this time, David, who knew a little about jazz from reading the Beat poets and writers, encouraged, "Just buy LPs, even if you don't know the musicians, that's how you'll learn."

When I stepped into Greenlaws, a small record store in Laconia, New Hampshire, and asked for Duke Ellington, the owner yelled to his assistant, "Hey, this kid wants some Duke!" handing me *Piano In the Background* and *Ellington Live at Newport, 1956*. The latter was an enormous hit. To do Paul Gonzalves' electrifying alto saxophone solo justice demanded repeated listening at high volume to the distress of any parent in earshot. Soon I outgrew Greenlaws' small inventory of jazz and began accompanying my father on buying trips to Boston. The musty smell of antique shops and used record stores became synonymous with discovery for both of us.

When I transitioned from the small grade school in Sanbornton, New Hampshire, to the larger high school in nearby Tilton, I'd hoped to find someone also interested in jazz, but had no success. My dyslexia and lack of interest or talent in sports, also made it difficult to fit in. Mostly I walked through the halls, from class to class, with an acute sense of alienation. Only Miles kept me from falling into self-indulgent pity. It was hard to be depressed with his toe-tapping music in my head. The few guys

I hung out with showed no interest in jazz, so I kept my mouth shut. What was the point?

Life took a turn for the positive when Miles' *Kind of Blue* showed up in the mailbox. That record threw gasoline on my smoldering curiosity in jazz, igniting a full-blown passion. The hypnotic sounds from Miles' trumpet and the power of John Coltrane's tenor sax riveted my attention. I played the album incessantly, gazing out my bedroom window, lost in the world of "Freddie Freeloader." I studied the liner notes like a Rosetta Stone for hidden clues about the music. I brought the record to my sophomore dance believing the kids would find it as mesmerizing as I did. Then I would be welcomed into the fold.

But what was I thinking? Could Miles dovetail with "Can't Help Falling in Love" or "Please Mr. Postman"?

The reaction was fast and furious: "Who put that crap on? Take it off!"

I guessed jazz was too esoteric for these knuckleheads. If I were in Boston, they would know what I was talking about.

In the summer of 1962, I spent much of my time in a small log cabin built by our family. A short walk from the house, we ran a line of electricity for lighting and, of course, the record player. Away from pressures to perform academically and socially, I reflected on the absurdity of my high school experience. With Miles and Coltrane as my companions, I looked out the window toward Boston and fantasized about living in the city. The summer ended too soon.

My contemporaries already viewed me as odd, but when I became a vegetarian on Easter Sunday, 1963, their reaction bordered on outright hostility. "What you don't understand, you distrust," was my only explanation. I bore their taunts, thinking they would become tired of the subject. Wrong! My mother didn't go for the idea either, annoyed it would complicate her limited culinary skills. She sought support from the family doctor: "From a health standpoint, there is no reason why Gerard should eat meat." I never regretted the decision. But while my strong views regarding diet and music helped strengthen my self identity, alienation increased. In the eyes of my classmates, I was a commie liberal; anyone who didn't eat burgers and listened to weird jazz must be a pinko.

Racial tension in the South began to surface on my horizon at this time. News reports made out that northern agitators, the so-called "Freedom Riders," were stirring up the Negroes. *It couldn't be that simple*, I thought. Before, the significance of Charles Mingus' "Fables of Faubus," (about the previous Governor of Alabama Orval Faubus and his racist political stance) or Billie Holiday's "Strange Fruit" (about lynching), had gone over my head. But when the present Governor of Alabama, George Wallace (*"segregation now, segregation tomorrow, segregation forever"*) unleashed dogs and water cannons on Negro protesters, I began to understand these musicians were confronting their audiences on race. Were Bill Evans, Dave Brubeck, and Herbie Mann—the only White musicians I cared for—doing the same thing?

In September 1963, the news of the bombing of the 16th Street Church in Birmingham, killing four Negro children, reached New Hampshire. This event was so horrific that the country, at last, took notice, with calls for President Kennedy to stop pussyfooting around racial issues and send federal troops to Alabama. The killing of innocent children boggled my mind. I found it impossible to understand the mentality behind this brutality. Such hatred ran chills down my spine wondering would I face the same bigotry when I moved to Boston?

Along with *Kind of Blue* and the cabin, another lifeline appeared—Rodney from Boston. Still making as many trips to the city with Dad as possible, my usual destinations were record stores and Hayes Bickford Cafeteria on Huntington Avenue and Gainsborough Street (Coffee Corner). My brother David had told me the last of the bohemians hung out there.

Comfortable sitting in front of a large window facing Huntington, Hayes Bickford Cafeteria wasn't the least bit threatening. I attempted to look the part, drinking a mug of coffee and eating a grilled cheese sandwich. While I was enjoying my after-meal Lucky Strike, a hip-looking Negro with a goatee pointed to the chair next to me. Both his size—six foot five—and dark complexion were intimidating. I did my best to look at ease.

Taking a seat, Rodney introduced himself and asked if I was from the neighborhood. As much as I wanted to believe he was sincere, who was he kidding? More questions followed.

"You know people on the Corner?"

"What are you looking for?"

"Why do you think there's something different here than in your place?"

My responses were typical teenage chatter, yet he found my yearning for the city and jazz curious. I vented about how square everybody was in high school, especially concerning music. He nodded. When I gathered enough confidence, I asked a question or two. As he replied, a sketchy picture emerged: his parents were in a band, always on the road, so his grandmother raised him. He skillfully left out his age, work, and where he now lived, adding to the mystery. His rhythmic gestures and expressions that I'd never heard before only increased my fascination. "Next time you're down, look me up," Rodney said. "You'll find me either at the Y, Coffee Corner, or the Lobster Claw. Just ask."

On the way home, our meeting replayed, raising questions: I shoulda' said this, shouldn't have said that, etc. But bumping into this older, much wiser urbanite was the most exciting thing that could have happened to me. Rodney being a different race added to the thrill, although I wasn't sure why. Back in high school, there was one lonely Negro, shunted up from the south to escape racial tension. There was nothing unusual about him other than the color of his skin. If there was such a thing as a Negro culture, this kid didn't exhibit it. Rodney's presence vibrated to a different beat, not just because of his age or the city. The difference was more primary, and I wanted to learn about it. Not to look a gift horse in the mouth, but why did he give me the time of day? What was my contribution?

The next time I saw Rodney, we picked up where we'd left off. Again, I complained about high school. First, he listened sympathetically, then shut it down by saying, "Look man, us Black folk have been dealing with lynching, police brutality, and every sort of discrimination imaginable ever since they dragged our Black asses out of Africa 350 years ago. Along the way, we've figured out a few things about survival. Dig what I'm sayin'?"

His directness about lynching and slaves raised my blood pressure. I didn't know where to look or what to say, overwhelmed by a subject I'd never spoken about, let alone to a Negro. I had little idea of what these people had suffered historically at the hands of Whites, but I knew enough to make me squirm. Reference to Blacks, not Negroes, was also a surprise. Until I could figure out the proper term to use, I avoided using either word. Black sounded proud, more masculine, but I waited for a clear sign.

Before I knew it, I'd asked him to spend a weekend in New Hampshire.

Rodney sat on the patio a month later, soaking up the sun and talking to my parents. My nonjudgmental father Dick, usually economical with his words, had a running dialogue with Rodney. My liberal mother Ruth, who had a passion for discussing literature or just talked to hear her own voice, especially with men, hovered around waiting for a way in. Rodney exhibited the same grace and confidence he had in Hayes Bickford. I went inside, then looked through the window to watch the unlikely scene: My middle-aged country parents chatting with this urban sophisticate. Ruth wore a modest sundress while Dick, dressed similar to a "beat" from a decade earlier, with long hair, a black turtleneck, jeans, and sandals. Many antique dealers were a breed unto themselves, free from society's norms. The scene could have been at a sidewalk cafe in Greenwich Village. When I went back outside, Ruth had shifted the topic to literature. She was impressed when they shared a similar taste in authors. Those few hours on the patio gave me a new appreciation for my parents' open-mindedness. They were more than polite; they appeared to genuinely like Rodney. After dinner, I drove him around. Besides the high school that he'd heard plenty about, there was little to see.

The following day, I asked how he slept. "Couldn't sleep a wink," he joked. "Too damn quiet up in here!"

The weekend had gone better than expected, but I wondered:

Why did I initiate the visit?

Did I want to show Rodney my parents weren't raving racists?

Was I looking for approval from them?

Why did Rodney agree to come up?

On the way to the bus station, I blurted out how at ease he seemed in Sanbornton.

"What? You think this is my first time I've stepped out of town or been around White people?"

I had no chance to rephrase. An excellent example of "Think before you speak."

He told a story about living with his grandmother who'd demanded he get out on the street and play with the Irish kids. She insisted, "I won't let you become one of those no-count niggers who never leaves the ghetto; you're gonna learn to deal with the reality of the street."

"Those kids used me as a punching bag 'til I'd had enough," Rodney said. "I ain't nobody's fool, ya dig? I waited til one of them was alone, then I kicked his Irish ass all the way down the block. Later on Gramma said, 'Guess what? Those kids' fathers are probably cops. Stay away from cops. They'd just a' soon shoot ya as not.'"

What I'm telling you is, I had to figure out how to survive, how to get over in this White America. It's a chess game, ya know? I learned chess as a child—a Black man living in America is the same game. 'Whites run the show,' Gramma said. 'Learn to navigate among them. Get on the inside.'"

I've had lots of White friends," Rodney said. "If they're real with me, I'm down with them.

So yes, I felt at ease with your people."

I wasn't sure if I was being dressed down, but clearly, "Black" was preferable to "Negro."

His intellect could move horizontally and vertically at once, then land right where it made the point. Following his stream of consciousness was surprisingly easy, similar to listening to jazz. What a welcome break from the tiresome antics of my schoolmates! High school could have sent me over the edge without the cabin and Rodney.

CHAPTER 2

THE HUB, THE ROAD, AND THE DRAFT

Halfway through my senior year, my friend Gary moved in with us in Sanbornton. Until then he'd been living at the local youth center because his single mom could not cope with her ever-increasing brood. He had a nervous way about him, continually flicking the ash off his cigarette while pushing the long hair out of his face as often as he flicked. Both of us couldn't leave New Hampshire soon enough. We were going to the Hub where I could breathe, pursue my passion for jazz, and look for like-minded friends. My parents' only stipulation was to find a decent place to live, and a job.

Gary and I rented an L-shaped room on the corner of Newbury and Fairfield Streets. There was nothing special about this part of the Back Bay. Mostly students and low-income renters, it was a far cry from Commonwealth Avenue. The best feature of our apartment was the second-floor bay window overlooking the street. Facilities were limited to a kitchenette built into the wall and a tiny bathroom. The cramped quarters, lack of money, and our inability to meet girls fueled tension between us. Gary routinely drank his paycheck up before the end of the week. As I ate my stewed tomatoes with cottage cheese and a peach, he'd put on a long face and say, "Aren't ya gonna share?" Hardened by an alcoholic older brother, I replied, "Maybe you should cut back on the beer, then you would have money for food." My careful budgeting to buy jazz records also annoyed him.

Luckily, before our animosity turned violent, two women from Brookline befriended us, not because we were so interesting—but because they were looking for a place to hang out in town. Jane had lovely dark hair, big brown eyes, and an air of self-confidence. Sherry, a tall strawberry blond, usually followed Jane's lead.

One evening Jane casually asked if we were interested in taking LSD. "It's still legal, you know."

Need you ask such a silly question?

"Hell, yeah!" We both said.

Sherry piped up, "You know who Richard Alpert (later known as Ram Dass) and Timothy Leary are? They live near me. Once I followed the curious parade of people who regularly visited their house, but I was immediately escorted out. One suggested I go to the Psychedelic Information Center (PIC) in Harvard Square."

She received pamphlets at the PIC, but no LSD. Determined, Sherry continued to visit the Center while Gary and I read whatever we could find on LSD in the public library. Finally, with six tabs in hand, Sherry rushed in with the good news. We planned to drop them over the weekend.

All week Gary and I could think of nothing else. Half-excited, half-scared, we couldn't imagine what to expect—except the unexpected. When the weekend arrived, Gary, Sherry, and I dropped, while Jane stayed straight in case of freakouts.

Soon, hallucinations morphed into reality while normalcy became an illusion. A chair that disappeared and reappeared seriously challenged my idea of what was tangible. On sensory overload, a bizarre world with alien emotions and perceptions enveloped me. With no fear, we embraced whatever came rushing in our direction. As Miles Davis' *Sketches of Spain* played, fluid colors emanated from the speakers. Time became flexible, nearly stopping, then leaping forward.

A universal current flowed through our little apartment that night as we adopted new personas to portray our heightened awareness. It picked me up and gave me a glimpse of the beyond. My sense of self—the little ego-self—merged into that current, showing me all things were possible if I let go. The whole of creation lay in front of me.

Before sunrise, Gary was under the impression that this powerful pharmaceutical was no longer affecting him.

"I wanna go out."

"Nothing doing," Jane said, "You're still too high." Then he started in about smelling fish.

"I'm telling you, I smell fish."

"Gary, enough with the fish."

"But I'm telling you, I really smell it."

An hour passed; sunshine beckoned at the curtains, and Jane suggested drawing them back. To our disbelief, right outside our window on Newbury Street stood a large parade float of Moby Dick.

"I told you. I told you I smelled fish!"

When Rodney stopped by to check on us, Gary didn't have much to say. I sensed that my intense friendship with Rodney was in decline that summer although I couldn't understand why. But strolling along the Esplanade one summer evening, everything became clear: Rodney suggested advancing our relationship through sex.

My god! I hadn't had sex with a woman yet.

Sex with a man had never crossed my mind.

Seeing the shock on my face, Rodney dropped the subject—temporarily.

For days I was consumed with his overture/proposal. Back in the boonies, being labeled gay was equivalent to death by a thousand cuts. Do's and don'ts defined acceptable behavior:

Never sit with your legs open.

Never wear a pink shirt.

Never carry a handkerchief.

The knee-jerk reaction to gay was, run!

Did I unknowingly encourage him? Why hadn't I figured out he was bisexual? Until now I had prided myself as nonconformist, but not when it came to sex. Our relationship looked doomed if one of us didn't relent, and I couldn't see that happening. Rodney's support had been a guiding beacon through the last torturous year of high school; the idea of losing him as a friend depressed me. But this was too much.

As summer turned into fall, I played a balancing act between sidestepping sex and not completely alienating Rodney. Our bond grew less intense, and our long talks reduced to a battle of wills. By winter we rarely saw each other.

Late in the summer, an English friend of my brother David landed in Boston looking for a place to stay. Leigh was our age. Gary and I were amused by the way he dressed, as if he expected an important visitor any moment. But his brimming self confidence was downright annoying. "You just got off the boat; what are you so cocky about?" But eventually, he won me over with his preference for jazz over pop or folk. When women heard his

English boarding-school accent, they asked if he knew the Beatles or the Stones. Hardly listening to the story he spun, their eyes would glaze over, and subconsciously they'd start unbuttoning their blouses. No wonder he was self confident. Gary and I had no such luck.

When Leigh asked why I was so passionate about Coltrane, I mentioned the profound effect of seeing him on television when I was 16. "Come down here!" David had called from our living room. "That guy you like on *Kind of Blue* is on TV." The John Coltrane Quartet played three pieces on the Jazz Casual Show: "Afro-Blue," "Alabama" (which I failed to connect to the bloody events from only a few months earlier), and "Impressions."

Witnessing the intensity of these musicians as they played, I grasped that jazz should be seen live. *Once I'm liberated from this outpost of civilization*, I dreamed, *I'll be a regular at the local jazz club.*

Leigh understood.

Two and a half years later, living in Boston, one day I walked past the Jazz Workshop. My eyeballs popped out when I saw the marquee: The John Coltrane Ensemble. I stopped so abruptly, someone ran into me from behind. What luck! After being in the city for only four months, Coltrane shows up. Pharoah Sanders on tenor and Rashied Ali on drums were part of the group. Racing back to tell Leigh," I shouted, "Coltrane's at the Workshop. We're going, right?"

"Of course!" he replied. I could think of nothing else other than seeing Coltrane that weekend.

On Friday, November 19, 1965, Leigh and I descended the stairs to the Workshop only to be confronted by the doorman. "Where do you think you're going? Let's see some ID."

The obstacle of being underage never occurred to us. Who wants to drink when Coltrane's in the room? I pleaded, "We've waited so long to hear Coltrane! We promise not to drink; please let us in."

For a moment, our chances seemed doubtful. Then an older couple behind us chided the doorkeeper, "They just want to see Coltrane; give 'em a break."

The doorkeeper grimaced. "All right, but I don't want to catch you ordering any booze. Got it?"

Stepping inside, the heavy odor of tobacco and stale beer nearly knocked us over. So this is what a jazz club smells like. Under normal circumstances, just being there would have been an event. But this was a whole different ball game. Leigh and I swaggered through the crowd of heavy-hitting jazz fans; definitely no room for squares. We congratulated ourselves with, "Yeah, we might be underage, but we made the scene."

The atmosphere crackled with excitement as the musicians crowded onto the small stage with their instruments (even bagpipes). When Coltrane entered, the audience fell silent, as did my racing mind. He had hardly put his horn to his mouth when Leigh and I looked at each other, knowing we were in deep water, unable to swim. I'd recently bought Coltrane's *Impressions* and *Live at Birdland*, but now the band was into a whole new bag. Their music started where most other jazz concludes. Coltrane and Pharoah soared, beckoning the universe to come down and manifest an alternate reality. Adrift, we floundered for something to hold on to, a theme, a phrase from *Impressions*, but no.

I was deaf to this music and dumb to the avant-garde, but I was not blind to Coltrane's aura. Coltrane seemed too large for the room, not his body, but his being. His extraordinary presence was more awe-inspiring than the music; something in me understood this was a man among men.

Halfway through the first set, Leigh suggested, "Go to the men's room; you'll walk right past Elvin (one of the drummers). Watch him."

Soaked in sweat, Elvin Jones embraced his drums so intently that he *became* the drums. His connection to every nuance of the music was mystical. Was his ability learned or God-given? Much the same as the ballet dancers Nureyev and Fonteyn, Elvin not only complemented but anticipated Trane's every twist and turn.

When I heard *Jazz Track* at ten, I recognized the language. That night at the Workshop, I recognized the language, but not the vocabulary.

Did Coltrane play just the mouthpiece?

When the musicians put their instruments down and disappeared off the stage, our "normal" sense of self slowly returned. We hesitated to leave, afraid the impact of the music would dissipate outside the club. Leigh and I walked out into the cool night air and watched the other patrons file out—some dazed, others energized, and more than a few displeased as they complained, "Why didn't he play the way he used to?" We wandered off to fathom what had happened, musically and otherwise. We assured ourselves that in time we'd be able to follow his music effortlessly.

Shortly after the concert, I read an article in *Downbeat* that stated, "The avant-garde, New Thing, or whatever you want to call it, isn't toe tappin' easy listening. It can press buttons, bringing up psychological issues that block the music from getting through. It takes self-confidence and letting go of preconceived notions to allow something new to flow into your being. The music is about beauty, maybe not the same as a rose, but beautiful nonetheless."

The Vietnam War dominated the news and our future plans. Gary and I would be called to serve "as sure as the sun rises." But just who were we serving? Our country didn't appear to be on the brink of disaster, so why were young Americans dying in Southeast Asia? I'd heard the old phrase: "yellow peril." What a country I lived in! If it wasn't those "lazy Blacks" threatening the American way, then the spread of "yellow peril" needed to be held in check.

The real question was what to do in the little time we had left.

In January 1966, with a Kerouac fantasy of pie-a-la-mode and Bird (alto saxophonist Charlie Parker) on the jukebox, Gary and I headed for the Mardi Gras and points West. (Leigh would join us when he scraped enough money together.) *The road is life*, I thought. But waiting for a ride in a snowstorm wasn't the life Kerouac talked about.

Hitchhiking through the South, many labeled us Northern agitators coming down to stir up the placid "negras." Gary's sardonic lip didn't help. In a Mississippi diner, we narrowly avoided a brawl that Gary had initiated by hustling out the back door.

New Orleans lived up to its reputation with booze, parades, and jazz. The only flaw in the days' long party was our roach-infested room way back of town.

In Scottsdale, we knocked on the door of an old friend of my Dad's. Sherb was an imposing, tall man with deep-set eyes hooded by the most enormous eyebrows I'd ever seen. So distracting were his dancing eyebrows that we missed what he was saying. His new, young wife reiterated that we were not welcome.

He dropped us off at a diner.

"Where can we stay?" I asked.

"Gee... whiz...boys, I wish I knew."

"Nothing? No suggestion?"

"Gee...whiz..."

Leigh, communicating through my parents, was expected to join us at Sherb's, so I told him, "A friend will be calling tomorrow; please tell him we'll be here, at this diner, waiting for him."

At closing time, the waiter recommended we go up to the Franciscan monastery that was within walking distance. "They'll take you in."

The monks were friendly and gave us a small but comfortable room. We were waiting for "Come pray with us, boys," but it never happened. They served a hearty breakfast in the morning, then dropped us back at the diner. At 3 pm, Leigh walked in with his blue blazer hung on a coat hanger trailing off his backpack. Who hitchhikes with a blue blazer?

Gary and I needed a break from each other, so I set off on my own. As a lonely hitchhiker, I knew sooner or later a man would pick me up with a proposition for sex. I wasn't shocked when it happened twice. Thankfully, they respected my "No thanks!" On the other hand, I was waiting for a ride with a woman who desperately wanted me—no such luck. I asked myself why gay men frightened me.

Was my sexual identity so fragile that someone could manipulate me?

If I had sex with men, would I be forever gay?

Was it a natural response?

The answer eluded me.

A week later, I found Gary and Leigh in the Hotel Roslyn next to the freight yard in San Diego. They had hooked up with a young runaway with a bag of speed. All three of them hadn't eaten, too paranoid to go out. The scene was right out of Billy Wilder's *Lost Weekend*. With his three-day growth and wild eyes, Leigh even looked similar to Ray Milland's character in the film. Gary was burning cigarette holes in the plastic curtains while keeping a sharp eye for any cops coming in their direction.

"What the hell's going on here? And who are you?" I said, pointing my finger at the cowering runaway. They were glad to see a fresh face and someone with enough sense to make them eat.

"They're watching the place," Gary said.

With unfamiliar authority, I replied, "Let 'em watch; we're leaving this room. NOW!"

Once we'd disentangled ourselves from the runaway, we headed to Long Beach where we landed jobs at a car wash and an apartment in a typical southern California complex centered around a swimming pool. Unfortunately my "California Dreaming" ended too soon with a notice from the draft board. Gary and Leigh gave me a proper send-off by renting a muscle car to drive to Las Vegas.

Since we didn't have money for gambling or showgirls, we had no reason to hang around in Vegas and continued to the Grand Canyon. What a driving marathon! But the spectacle of the Canyon made our long ordeal worthwhile.

San Francisco was the mecca for all young East Coasters and I was determined to see it before taking part in "this man's army," so they dropped me in Malibu on Route 1—a perfect spot to start hitchhiking. The goodbyes were sober; Gary knew his call to serve would be coming soon and Leigh wondered about his next move.

Frisco was beautiful with hippies everywhere, but I was too freaked out to appreciate the scene. I chose to sit in an all-night movie theater, smoking cigarettes and watching *The Ipcress File* repeatedly.

The long trip back to New Hampshire was a blur.

As I prepared for the inevitable, Uncle Bob, who had served during WW2, suggested cutting my long hair before the induction.

"Your hair is coming off anyway. Now the Army won't identify you as a hippie troublemaker."

There I stood, skinny, with pimples on the back of my neck and a lumpy, bumpy skull, ready for the Army. But why was I passively going off to kill or be killed? People were applying for conscientious objector status or fleeing to Canada. Why not me? What a disappointment to myself and others, complying without a protest. My brain was malfunctioning. This would be a concern in normal circumstances, but all I could manage was to go with the flow.

The day came: May, Friday the 13th, 1966. *A fitting date*, I thought. All the draftees were in a daze entering the large examination hall in Manchester The induction exam only consisted of a humiliating check for hemorrhoids, then a brief chat with a doctor. When I entered the doctor's office, he did a double take.

Peering into my face, he asked, "Is anything bothering you?"

A light switched on in my feeble brain. *There is a chance here; don't screw it up.*

"Well, ever since I moved away from my mother, I've been feeling depressed."

"Depressed? What do you do about that?" he wanted to know.

"I drink Renolgren."

"Renolgren, what is that? I've never heard of it." He was puzzled.

"It's a nose spray. I squirt it into water and drink it," I said with a poker face.

The Doctor took out his pen and began to write. *This could be good*, I told myself, *but be cool, don't overdo it.*

Looking sternly at me, he asked, "Have you taken hallucinogens? LSD?"

"Twice."

More writing. "What other drugs have you taken?

"Well, I smoke cigarettes and..."

"No! DRUGS." The Doctor said.

"Marijuana?"

"Yes."

"I often smoke a little at bedtime so I can sleep."

"You don't sleep?"

"No. Am I in trouble? My mother told me to behave myself," I said, trying my best to feign innocence.

"No son, you're not in trouble, but the Army will not need your service at this time."

"Why not?"

"You never mind that for now." He gave me a 1Y classification; the Army could call me at a later date.

"Oh," I said, looking at the floor. "I'm so sorry to be a disappointment."

I could hardly contain myself. I wanted to kiss the guy and do cartwheels out the door.

They gave me a bus ticket back home. I was out of the Army for the foreseeable future. On the bus ride, my head started spinning again—but in the opposite direction. An unknown future tempered my sense of relief. For the past six weeks, I had believed life as I knew it would end on Friday the 13th, and I had made no plans for a different outcome

Back in Sanbornton, I couldn't readjust; nothing felt right. Treading water, I took a factory job in nearby Laconia. The graveyard shift paid better, and using the family car at night wouldn't interfere with my parent's daytime need of the car.

As expected, Gary received his draft notice. After I related my story, he acted cocky about beating the system. Unfortunately, *his* story didn't fly. He began by volunteering too much information, saying he had taken drugs.

The abrupt response was, "Not anymore!"

"I'm gay."

"Not anymore!"

After boot camp, he came up for a visit. The transformation into a soldier was well underway and it frightened me. Gary was going to Vietnam.

Adjusting to the graveyard shift left me exhausted, adding to my disorientation. The only bright spot came through the car radio on the way to work. Ed Beach's *Just Jazz* from Rochester, NY, treated me to his hip selection. On the job, talk radio played in the background. Once or twice I heard someone call my name, jerking me from my stupor of tracking ball-bearing production. How was that possible? Was the company hacking into the radio, calling out employees' names to keep them alert? My anxiety skyrocketed. After only six weeks at the factory, I checked myself in at the state mental hospital in Concord, New Hampshire.

The Walker ward wasn't the snakepit horror scene I'd expected. Student nurses arrived every morning with short white skirts and white stockings to lift our spirits. In group therapy, I soon learned to keep quiet to avoid becoming the subject of the sessions. Usually some poor guy namely Duffy, who'd suffered too many shock treatments, became the target. He shaved off his eyebrows one morning, then caught hell in Group. Another patient who'd been caught masturbating at night became the target. After watching patients with *real* problems and those who were institutionalized, I quickly realized my difficulty boiled down to an appalling attitude. But how to extricate myself from the mess I'd created by coming here? The hospital was grossly understaffed; it could be weeks before I'd see a doctor again.

My parents arranged for a local psychologist to assist in the release process, and the following week I was out. Renewed with a clear idea of what I needed to do, I started bimonthly sessions with the psychologist. On my first meeting with Dr. McKay, I explained that the time spent in the nuthouse had been very constructive. Other than needing a serious attitude adjustment, my life was fine, I told him. I continued to see McKay for the next eight months.

PART TWO

ANDERSON STREET

CHAPTER 3

THE WIGMAN

Because of my dyslexia, college was never an option, so in the fall of 1966 I enrolled in the Northeast Institute of Technology (NIT) on the backside of Beacon Hill in Boston. When I visited the school during the summer, the array of characters on the street and the anything-goes vibe assured me I could manage coming to the city alone. I remembered the trauma of leaving the local grade school for the neighboring town's high school without knowing a soul. That didn't work out so well, but let's not confuse Tilton, New Hampshire, with Beacon Hill. The area resembled a miniature Haight Ashbury, with freaks on nearby Cambridge Street as common as fleas on a dog—some stoned, others panhandling, chicks with patchouli oil and beads handing out free copies of the *Real Paper* and the *Phoenix*. The Boston Brahmins were not amused as the hippies paraded through Louisburg Square to the Boston Common for free rock concerts, protests, or smoke-ins. Other than scoring some grass and watching the hippie chicks, the rock concerts and the protests weren't big attractions for me.

NIT provided a dormitory of sorts one street up from the school. The imposed restrictions pinched. My single room was the size of a shoebox, too small for my stereo. Surrounded by nerds, dorm life required an adjustment.

Within the first week at NIT, I met a kindred spirit. Steve was a day student from Roxbury, a sharp-looking hipster with an easy-going manner, espresso-brown skin, a short afro, and big black glasses that needed constant adjustment. He stood out, older and wiser than the mostly suburban kids just out of high school. I introduced myself as Gerard, but when he heard my last name, he said, "No man, you're Wig, the Wigman."

Noticing the roach burns on his thumb, I made the motion of smoking. "Oh yeah," he said, "the herb and I are old friends."

Steve could talk. He could spin out a tale for hours, but personal matters didn't come up. He focused on the here and now, which usually meant school, music and who he could seduce. Fortunately, my fiasco with Rodney didn't prejudice me against having a Black friend. Initially, I followed his lead, saying little about my background or what I was thinking, but I slowly nudged the conversation toward a more personal direction. Steve hesitated to invite me to his "crib" despite knowing how anxious I was to leave the dorm and hang out. Being White presented some complications. First, I had to show hipness, ability to handle myself in the ghetto. But how to do that without going there? The idea of crossing the "border" excited me. I felt ready to stick my neck out with Steve close at hand. What would I find? How different could it be? An air of mystery surrounded Roxbury, an unknown territory for most Whites. When I was a child, if my parents told me I couldn't go here or there, I wanted to go all the more. Going to Roxbury was the same, but I had to wait until Steve was good and ready.

"Okay, Wigman," he finally said one day, "Let's go to the Berry."

Not sure where the Berry was, I agreed, "Yeah, man, let's do it."

We rode the "El" (elevated train) up front, looking out the portal down the tracks. As we rattled above Washington Street, Steve pointed out landmarks: the Red Fez, the Puritan movie theater, and pawn shops. The train snaked its way into Dudley Square, a massive station high above the street where buses departed to all points. The slate roof, intricate ironwork, and impressive balustrade spoke of a period when cities took pride in public buildings. Despite the deteriorating condition, I imagined Paddington or Waterloo stations in London to look similar. My Victorian fantasy quickly vanished as I descended into the half-light below where an intimidating crowd loitered, their eyes following me like a shadow. I saw men in slick outfits with expressions that said, "I've got whatever you want, my man." Steve noticed my hesitating stare and said, "Pay 'em no mind." Another group had a different vibe: "Whatever *you* got, I want it." Steve later spelled out the need of many folks in the ghetto to have a hustle on the side to make ends meet. "Life's a struggle here; you have to make opportunities even when there aren't any."

With adrenaline pumping, my first steps into the ghetto confirmed the notion of sticking my neck out. I had rushed to the city to find what was lacking in the safety and predictability of country life. Here in Roxbury, would I find some of the missing pieces? As Dorothy said: "We're not in Kansas anymore."

I asked about those sharp-dressed men.

"Pimps."

Wow, pimps! Then where are those mythical beauties with love for sale? *Stay focused*, I told myself. *Don't blow your maiden voyage to the ghetto by spacing out.* Walking up Roxbury Street, there was little traffic and fewer pedestrians. Without a single tree to break the monotony of the dusty sidewalk, a Ray Charles song came to mind, "I'm Gonna Move to the Outskirts of Town."

Highland Street, where Steve lived, branched out of Eliot Square. A white Colonial church dominated the small park. Passing the corner convenience store, I slowed my pace to see what was on display in the window. A small selection of fruit and vegetables grew less appetizing the closer I looked, old and tired, flies buzzing around. Wholesalers knew where to unload their scraps down in the ghetto. *How do people raise a healthy family on the dregs?* I guessed it was possible; Steve was fit.

The famous Fort Hill Tower in the distance caught my eye. Back in the 1870s, it stored water for the local Roxbury community. It resembled the Gothic tower where the wicked witch Mother Gothel had imprisoned Rapunzel. One side of Highland Street introduced me to my first empty city block—nothing but weeds and trash. On the other side stood a row of modest Victorian single-family homes, now broken into apartments, all desperately needing repair. I'd seen old, dilapidated houses in the country—my uncle had bought one to restore, the only one in the town—but to see an entire city block empty or in disrepair shocked me. What a waste! Why doesn't the city build housing for the poor? I questioned. Maybe it served as a dumping ground for low-income/no-income people with rundown houses, a wasted economy, and little hope. During our 20-minute walk from the train, I'd seen one contradiction after another: the aging Victorian station, a Colonial church, a gothic tower, and a wasteland. The Boston I knew was nowhere in sight. The sun, the blue sky, and the air we breathe were the same, but that's where the similarity ended.

When we reached 25 Highland, just up from the Square, Steve pointed to the dormers on the third floor, saying that was his crib—"the penthouse."

The stress of my initial foray into the Black neighborhood peaked at the thought of entering a Black household. What if the family were as racist as so many White people were? The headlines would read: *Unidentified Young White Male Found Lynched in Eliot Square*. But I kept my cool, knowing my hipness was on trial. I calmed down when no one greeted us in the large unfurnished hallway. We went straight up to his sanctuary. Still feeling weak-kneed, I crashed on the couch to gather my composure. Putting myself through all this anxiety called into question if it was worthwhile. There would be time to reflect later; right now, I wanted to convince Steve I was worthy of being in his crib.

The owners, Willa Mae and Willa Bee, lived on the first two floors along with Steve's mother, Ernestine, who rented a room. We became acquainted over subsequent visits, the hippest mother I'd ever met. She'd invite me to chat while I waited for her chronically late son. Willa Mae and Willa Bee didn't mind me coming by either, although they made it clear that standing on the porch with the overhead light on wasn't a good idea.

"Edison ain't no friend of mine," Willa Mae said one night, turning the light off (though I suspect the real reason was she didn't want the neighbors to see "Whitey" on the porch).

Steve's living room was all about hearing the music with speakers placed for maximum effect. A well-broken-in couch and easy chair were positioned to catch even the subtlest tones. A coffee table covered with marihuana stems and seeds and a clip of Zig Zag papers helped me feel at ease. Incense lingered in the air. Steve went into the other room while I idly looked out the window at the empty lots. The yellowed paper window shade was so fragile I dared not touch it. All this meant little when my eyes landed on the stack of jazz records next to the amplifier. Art Blakey, Lee Morgan, and Hank Mobley (Mobley's

"The Vamp '' was Steve's theme song and nickname) all stared at me.

"Oh shit!" I exclaimed.

"What?" He said from his bedroom.

"Jazz! You're into jazz."

"Does the sun rise in the East?" He asked, coming through the door with a grin. "You down with the music?"

"I've always been attracted to it but couldn't hear much in New Hampshire, ya know? Put something on."

He flared up a joint. "For your listening pleasure, we will now hear Art Blakey's "The Egyptian." Please feel free to express yourself openly here at the 'House of Progressive Jazz.' Tips are graciously received after the show."

I flicked through his collection as Art Blakey pounded out a heavy beat.

Seeing my positive reaction, he turned up the volume. The hair on my arms stood up in response to Wayne Shorter's blistering tenor solo. "Man, that's a smoker! What else?"

"You just sit back and dig; there's plenty more, m'man." The maestro was in his element.

My stereotype of Blacks and jazz being one and the same found no contradiction in Steve. Of course, I had enough sense to keep such myths to myself.

"You always been into jazz?" I asked.

"Since junior high. My best friend Kenny hipped me to jazz. It was all about jazz, jazz, jazz at his place. He hung out with Tony Williams. You know who Tony is, right? Miles Davis' drummer? Tony got Kenny into the music."

"You knew Tony?"

"Hell, yeah! Another success story from the Berry. He's older, but we hung out. Anyway, every time I went to Kenny's, he'd turn me on to another musician. I dug it from the start."

The sun had long since set, the couch was seductively comfortable, the great music continued, and with a buzz going, how could I trudge back to Dudley? When I made noise about heading out, Steve said it wasn't a good idea. "Without me, you shouldn't be on the street this late, and I sure as hell ain't going out now. Just relax, your dorm ain't goin' nowhere and neither are you."

His insistence that I should stay boosted my confidence. He wouldn't be asking some square to crash; I settled back in the glow of making the grade.

That evening previewed the future. Many nights would be spent listening to music until the early hours, then crashing on the couch. Steve made me perfectly comfortable hanging in the ghetto. As we got to know each other better, I probed for his views on poverty and race. Steve's world *did* appear different, so if I wanted to understand humanity on a larger scale, this was an excellent place to start. *Just listen and observe*, I advised myself. *Their knowledge could become part of mine.*

On one lazy afternoon, Steve suggested, "Let's walk up to Fort Hill and cop a few of those White chicks living there."

"Never mind the White chicks," I said. "What about some brown sugar?"

"Oh no, not that; you ain't ready for no brown sugar."

I'd only had one short sexual affair, when I'd first moved to Boston, with a young woman as naive as myself. Venturing into deep waters with a streetwise Black woman would have to wait.

One weekend, as I ascended the stairs to the third floor, I heard Coltrane echoing down the hall. The music was so loud Steve didn't notice me standing in the doorway. He sat in the overstuffed chair in the middle of the room, with speakers at each end, eyes closed and head bobbing to Coltrane's "Africa." I'd heard the LP before, but seeing Steve carried away in the stream of this musical odyssey opened my ears further.

The initial pulsing bass line is the hook. Then the orchestra (17 pieces augmenting Coltrane's classic quartet) slowly enters, creating color and texture before Coltrane begins his foray. As the tenor takes flight, the big band adds a further dimension to Coltrane's commentary with occasional bursts throughout his solo. After the solo, the orchestration fades in and out as McCoy Tyner's piano lays out the base color before taking center stage, pounding out a simple but powerful solo accompanied by the bass duo of Reggie Workman and Art Davis and Elvin Jones' drums. This section concludes with the orchestra laying the ground for the master's re-entry with rising and falling African sounds enhancing the saxophone's cry until Coltrane finds resolution. Leaning against the doorway, I now understood; you don't just *listen* to "Africa;" you *experience* it.

When Steve returned to the here and now, we looked at each other and shook our heads. Finally, he said, "That's some heavy shit! You dug it, right?"

Steve appreciated that I needed advice on street smarts. Back in New Hampshire, there was no need for such things. My hometown didn't have gangs, hustlers, pimps, or even sidewalks. All good for growing up, but boring for this young adult.

"Always know who is behind you, in front, and on the side of you. If you feel the least bit uncomfortable, go into a store or cross the street. Don't hesitate," Steve said. "Follow your gut. And walking up from Dudley, if somebody says, 'Hey you,' they're not talking to you, right? Just keep walking, don't engage with anybody."

A week later, halfway to Steve's, I heard, "Hey. Hey man, what's happening?" from across the street.

Head lowered, I increased my pace. Again, "Hey, hold up."

Just before breaking into a sprint, I heard, "Wigman, it's me, Steve!"

A few weeks later, My father was in Boston on business and picked me up on the Hill. Since Steve was with me, I insisted we give him a ride home. Dad wasn't pleased about the detour, but I told him, "I'll drive, I know the way."

When we dropped him off, Dad caught sight of the waste-land across the street and frowned. Pulling away, he said, "I had no idea."

"What do you mean?" I said, wanting to hear his take on urban blight.

"I just didn't realize Negroes lived in such poor conditions."

Even though he grew up poor in rural Vermont, he'd never experienced urban poverty. The rest of the ride back to New Hampshire was silent.

A growing angst about meeting Steve's home crew overshadowed my visits. Even though he was at ease with me in his crib, would his partners go along with Whitey in the room? My tendency to worry often proved unwarranted, spoiling the moment with endless what-ifs. In my early days visiting Highland Street, a close friend of his, Earl, better known as Chops, stepped into the room with authority. Well-dressed, trimmed hair, and with the same complexion as Steve, his hard-boiled muscular appearance made up for his short stature. Without acting outright hostile, he didn't say anything to me. I tried to act laid back, but my stomach instantly knotted. Then the thought hit me: *I could be the first White man in Steve's house, catching Chops off guard.*

"Chops, this is the Wigman; he's also going to NIT."

Chops replied in a slightly confrontational tone, "Oh yeah, where you from?"

"Beacon Hill."

"You're from the Hill?"

"The dorm is."

"No, man, not the dorm. Where you come from, your people?"

"Up in New Hampshire."

I glanced at Steve, but his expression told me I was on my own. Looking at me, Chops challenged, "Bet you didn't hear no jazz up in there?"

I doubted he was interested in a long story about *Jazz Track* and *Kind of Blue*, so I gave him an abridged version of listening to Miles at ten. His comment was: "Now ain't that some shit! You're up in the woods listening to Miles and Coltrane, while it took me a long time to get hip to the music right here in the ghetto. You've got some big ears to hear all that music at ten; the gods must have smiled on you."

With a slight grin, he asked, "Who else beside Miles and Trane are you into?"

I rattled off Ellington and Mingus without getting much response.

"Well, Lee—Lee Morgan's my main man," Chops said. "Sure, Miles can play, but Lee, he knows how to burn the joint down."

Steve encouraged me to tell Chops about seeing Coltrane and Pharoah Sanders.

"You saw Trane, with Phaa–row? Shooot! You was in some deeep water."

Music was a safe subject to stick to. During a lull, I asked how he'd discovered jazz.

"Right here in this room! I was a drinking man into R&B, right? I knew I had to change up when I checked Steve and his partner Kenny, smokin' reefer, all mellow, listening to Coltrane. Trane was saying something deep, a whole different bag than R&B."

A ceremonial joint was passed around as if confirming acceptance of a social order. I was in. My nerves faded, and I reveled in the approval. The afternoon passed with jokes, jazz, and reefer. Before dark, I grabbed my coat to go. "Hold up, Wigman," Chops said, "I'll go with you." Meeting one of Steve's friends had gone remarkably well.

The following weekend found me right back on Highland Street, in the groove with Steve and Chops. Since Steve grew up in Roxbury, I asked Chops if he was a native of the Berry as well. In a low voice, he muttered, "Yup."

Steve nudged him, "Go on, man. Tell him where you were born."

Chops had entered the world in a cotton field in Mississippi, his mother barely sixteen. Unable to care for him, she shipped Chops off to the "grandparents" in Boston. Five years later, she joined her son, carrying a newborn.

What decade—what century—are we talking about? Born in a cotton field to a sixteen-year-old? I said nothing for fear of showing my disbelief. *You see,* I said to myself, *life in the ghetto is full of surprises. Wonder if his childhood messed with his head?*

Then he explained that his mother had become a Jehovah's Witness. Being dragged from door to door, handing out leaflets, was too embarrassing for a young man making his way on the mean streets. The experience convinced him all religions were fairy tales.

After high school, Steve and Chops worked to save for college, desperate to avoid the draft or get stuck in the ghetto. Agriculture & Technology College in Greensboro, NC, accepted both of them. Before leaving, Steve's father made a rare appearance to wish him farewell. "Oh, by the way, if you order soup down south," the father instructed, "don't ask for crackers; ask for soda biscuits. You don't want to piss off the White folk."

After a year and a half, with poor grades and little money, Chops was back in Boston looking for another way to avoid the draft. Steve followed at the end of the term, then enrolled at NIT that fall.

Chops' tough exterior was just that—exterior. One evening, his genuine concern for me showed as we walked down Highland Street past the corner store. With barely a streetlamp in the square, the light from the store cast long shadows of the toughs hanging outside. A barrage of racial slurs rang out when they caught sight of me.

"Now, what the fuck is Whitey doin' here?"

My body went so rigid, walking like the Tin Man. *I'm in deep shit now*, I rebuked myself.

Hanging around in Roxbury, what was I thinking, that I was blending in? Fool! And now my White ass is going to cause Chops grief.

"Keep moving," Chops whispered as he turned to confront them. "If you're talking to him, you're talking to me. Do you have something else to say?"

Out of earshot, a sense of shame consumed me. If those punks attacked Chops, how much help would I be down the street? If the tables were turned, would I confront the bigots?

Chops quickly joined me, laughing, saying they were just a bunch of punks with nothing better to do than call out Whitey.

"Man, I feel so guilty for walking away."

"You did the right thing. You're in the Berry now; there's no shame in stepping back when there's no way forward. Fighting ain't your bag anyway."

Chops proved himself to be a man of substance that night. On the train ride back to the Hill, most of the Black men looked menacing, the same as the toughs on the corner. I wondered if a White man with Black friends in the ghetto always stirred up hostility. Until now, unconsciously, I acted on the premise that if I had no problem with African-Americans, they would have no problem with me. That type of thinking comes from privilege, which I took for granted. If privilege is systematically denied from birth, who wouldn't be angry?

CHAPTER 4

THE APARTMENT UPSTAIRS

J ust before I started classes at NIT, Leigh and his girlfriend Vickie moved into 16 Anderson Street, right down from Northeast Institute. I now had two places to escape the confines of the dorm—weeknights at Leigh and Vickie's and weekends at Steve's. Insensitive to Leigh and Vickie's need for privacy, however, I quickly became a pain in the neck. One evening, in a not so subtle attempt to get rid of me for a while, Leigh suggested I go to the apartment on the third floor and introduce myself.

Missing the point, I said, "Why? Do you know this guy up there?"

"Be big for once. Just go up and see," Leigh taunted.

I felt shy about knocking on a stranger's door. What would I say? *This must be some kind of joke*, I thought as the door flew open after my first knock. A Black man about my age, with bulbous eyes framed by tortoise-shell glasses and ears too big for his head, greeted me with a huge toothy smile. "Hey, what's happenin'?"

All I could say was, "Do you have any matches?"

He quickly noticed the tell-tale roach burns on my thumb and resembling a salute from a secret society, he showed me the same marks on his.

"Oh, just come on in," he said, with a raucous laugh.

As soon as I crossed the threshold, a sense of déjà vu overwhelmed me. It had nothing to do with the apartment resembling Vickie's, it was something more subtle than that. But this was hardly the time to space out on some inexplicable sensation, so I refocused. He motioned for me to sit down as he went to his stereo. As soon as I landed on the couch, I had a sense of belonging. At first glance, nothing unusual stood out. Then I caught sight of a large stack of records glowing brighter than a beacon. Charles Mingus' *Mingus Presents Mingus* in front of the pile of LPs came as no surprise, again confirming my assumption that all Blacks were jazz fans. The afternoon sun flooded through the windows as we settled back and listened to Freddie Hubbard's *Blue Spirit*.

"You mind if I look through your LPs?"

When I saw that most of his collection was jazz, the real deal, I exclaimed, "I can't believe this; you have a better selection than most record stores!"

"Always dug the music, started buying them around twelve or so. You into it? What do you want to hear?"

"Oh no, Freddie Hubbard is fine."

As the music played, he asked, "So, who do you listen to?"

This could be good, I thought. *If I don't come across as a lame country boy, he might teach me about jazz.*

"Well, mostly Miles and Coltrane, and also…"

Suddenly, a serious expression replaced his smile. Shit, what have I stepped into now?

"Coltrane? That's a hallowed name in this house. Glad you're hip to him. What Trane LPs do you have?"

Since my collection wasn't much to brag about, I jumped into the story about seeing Coltrane with Pharoah Sanders a year ago. That would impress him more than my few records.

"Say what? You saw Trane with two drummers *and* Phaa-row. Shit!" he said, dropping Coltrane's *Crescent* on the turntable. "You witnessed a moment that won't be repeated, just too heavy for most folks." He plopped down beside me saying, "Born and raised here and I didn't make it to see Coltrane with Pharoah. And you, just in town, knew enough to catch that blistering group! That just goes to show the universal appeal of Coltrane."

Once again, my Coltrane story evoked the same astonishment as it had with Chops, confirming how fortunate I was to have been in his presence. I hadn't realized it would give me instant credibility. As a newcomer to Anderson Street, Highland Street, and jazz, anything that cast my character in a better light was a good thing.

I didn't want to overstay my welcome, so I pulled myself off the couch to say goodbye. I experienced the same sense of undefined familiarity as I approached the door. Grasping for an explanation, I attributed it to the similar vibe at Steve's with the music and the reefer. But this was more complex, like an ancient memory from a past life flickering into my subconscious. What I could be sure of was when Bobby opened his door and asked me in, I entered a new phase of my life.

I couldn't wait to go back for more music and Bobby. A pretty woman let me in when I knocked on his door that weekend. He'd failed to mention his girlfriend Toni. This full-figured woman with black wavy hair, soft mocha skin, and sparkling eyes rendered me speechless. I struggled to keep my eyes from following the plunging neckline to her cleavage. She noticed my reaction and faintly smiled. Frozen in my tracks, I could feel my blood pressure rising. That wouldn't be the only thing rising if I didn't divert my attention quickly.

Bobby piped up, "This is Gerard. He's attending the trade school on the corner, but he's more interested in the music."

Breaking into a full smile, she said, "Well, come on in. Bobby has a first-class collection. Come up anytime."

Watching Toni speak, her white teeth surrounded by full lips, made it impossible to focus on what she said. Before I could thank her, she walked toward the kitchen with her hips swaying. Pushing my eyeballs back in place, I turned to Bobby with an apology. He laughed, nodding his head. My ogling hadn't offended him. So much time had passed since I'd been intimate with a woman that Toni's beauty and sexuality were overpowering, leaving me feeling inadequate. All I could say was, "Damn!"

As I had hoped, Bobby was eager to enlighten me on all things jazz. He suggested "listening sessions" once or twice a week. "We'll do it before Toni returns from work—limit the distractions." Speaking of work, I briefly wondered what he did, but it seemed irrelevant at the time. Being in the present was enough.

"Listening session?" I asked.

"Yeah, just music, no hanging out or getting high. Ya know, like going to class," Bobby said.

"I could get into that. Great idea!" I exclaimed.

The following day, records of the featured musician lay on the coffee table. "Take a look at these. Today, we're listening to the great drummer Chico Hamilton and his smokin' band."

Bobby made no further explanation. *Man, this is serious as a heart attack; I'd better pay attention if I want to learn about this music*, I told myself.

After playing a few sides, he asked my opinion. That first day I felt too intimidated to offer much of a comment, but as the sessions continued, I slowly began to voice my opinion, confident in the safe environment he had created. No matter how inane my comments were, he never belittled what I said. Having heard the term "guru" in another context, I thought the title fit Bobby: "Jazz Guru."

In no time, Bobby and I acted as if we'd known each other for a decade. But the same concerns I had over at Steve's worried me. How would Bobby's friends react to seeing "white on rice" in the room?

Arthur was the first. His dark complexion, unkempt short afro, and clean but crumpled clothes gave him a bohemian air. As he walked in, self-assured, his glance in my direction was oblique. *Shit*, I thought, *he's got an attitude*. Like a dog encountering the alpha male, I kept my head lowered. Bobby bounced around the room, arms waving to the music, then, like a fluttering butterfly, he settled next to me on the couch.

"Arthur, this is Wigman. He's goin' to the trade school up on the corner, but the real reason he's down from the country is to hear the music. And dig it; he saw Trane with Pharoah and Rashied in the band at the Workshop last fall."

Arthur peered over his glasses, making an approving gesture, then said, "Trane and Pharoah? Were you ready for that?"

As the words *Hell yeah* formed, I stopped myself, thinking there was no need to be cocky. My intimidation faded, watching him bobbing to the music. That first look meant nothing, just surveying the scene. A simple answer would do. "No, not in the least. I'd been listening to *Impressions* and *Live at The Village Vanguard*, but as good as they are, what he's doing now is something else.

The music escaped me, but Coltrane's presence didn't. He struck me as a man who knew something out of the ordinary. I don't know what, but I'll never forget being in the same room as him."

"Yeah, man, Trane, he knows what we need to know," Bobby said as Arthur raised his eyebrows thoughtfully.

Arthur attended Boston University, majoring in psychology. With free tuition, because his mother was a librarian at BU, he didn't have to work and had plenty of time to hang out after classes. Besides his political views, he enlightened us in vivid detail about all the mini-skirted White chicks anxious to be laid by a Black buck. Bobby and I commiserated on his heavy burden. He had a talent for spinning a tale in such detail that one could easily imagine being there. I suggested he could illustrate movie storyboards if the psychology didn't work out.

Coltrane's *Olé* was a favorite of ours, but watching Arthur become theatrical as the intensity built in the piece was as exciting as the music. When the energy approached a boiling point, Arthur would jump up, mount his imaginary chariot and crack his whip to fly away! When the crescendo finished, so did he, collapsing back in the chair. Peering over his glasses with a smile, he'd say, "Yes, siree!"

There was no escaping the uncertainty in our country at this time. Arthur expressed his frustration about the sociopolitical environment more than the rest of us. He brought up a recent report in the *Boston Globe* about a White cop beating a Black driver who'd been passing through the tony suburb of nearby Wellesley. Stopped for a broken taillight, a confrontation ensued, ending with the driver bloodied and in jail. Arthur ranted, Bobby made appropriate responses, and I kept quiet. Best thing for me to do was just listen. Eventually, Bobby passed a joint to Arthur, which had the desired effect of lowering the temperature. With Arthur's talent for oratory and his sardonic view of politics, I foresaw more rants in the future. Fortunately, his humor helped lift the weight off heavy subjects. Yet I wondered if his humor was a deflection.

Dos came in with Arthur a few days later. He was a large, jovial guy with a light beige complexion with his hair in a "do" (straightened). The "process" looked dated and didn't suit his easy-going manner. He spoke in almost a drawl and made me think his people were from the deep South. Dos came right over and asked me what was happening; I was relieved there was no sign of attitude. When he heard I dug the alto saxophonist Jackie McLean, he said, "Gee-rhaa, let's hear some JMac right now."

Hard bop was his first choice in jazz, but he was also into Coltrane and other tenor players from the avant-garde, mainly Archie Shepp and Pharoah Sanders. Unlike Bobby and Arthur, he didn't talk that much, and what he did say revealed little. Watching these old friends relate together, I was eager to be included in the same way.

The bond between the three of them was so tight that I could trip over it if I wasn't careful. I figured their shared experience in the neighborhood explained the camaraderie, but through listening to their stories, another explanation emerged. Suffering from every type of century-old discrimination united them in a fight against oppression. All Blacks were brothers and sisters in the struggle. A knowing glance between them said more than words, reminding me how my father and uncle (identical twins) usually communicated.

Mainly, my friends dealt with the burden of their skin color remarkably well. Frustration and resentment could still erupt over what seemed to me a minor infraction which, to them, reinforced the denial to participate in the so-called American dream.

During the summer of 1966, lost in my drama of being rejected from the military and what was coming next, I had missed hearing about the race riots in Chicago's West Side with angry Puerto Ricans battling police for days. Then came Cleveland, where four died during the six-day melee between the police and Blacks. The Brooklyn disturbance between Blacks and Puerto Ricans wasn't as deadly as Cleveland; nevertheless, it resulted in massive property damage to the Bedford-Stuyvesant area. Now it was 1967 and both Bobby and Arthur agreed that in spite of all the riots, how little had changed and they expressed their irritation with our do-nothing government. Fortunately, Bobby was able to discuss racial issues without becoming overheated as Arthur often could do. I needed to be better informed to keep up with the discussion.

"What's fueling the tension between Blacks and Whites now?" I naively asked.

"It's both simple and complicated," Bobby said. "Simple because we're only asking for what every citizen of America wants—the chance to follow their destiny. Complicated because there's always been a White man saying, 'No, no. Not yet. You boys aren't ready.' To change the mindset of superiority isn't child's play. And to forgive the centuries of unspeakable brutality carried out on us ever since 1619 is no small thing either."

"1619?"

"That's when the first slaves were sold by pirates to Jamestown. They don't teach that in American history, do they?"

Bobby paused to rifle through his record collection for the appropriate soundtrack and continued, "In the early '60s, many believed civil rights marches and voter registration could make a difference. But they didn't. Nothing would change without a fight. When the cops came in, wailing their billy clubs and using water cannons to put down a demonstration, the community said, 'Okay, if that's the way you want to play, we can do that too.' How many beatings does it take before you say, fuck it, I'm fighting back? Most of the violence today is White cops on Blacks. There's no love lost between the Whites and Blacks, but it's the cops who enforce racist policies and keep the status quo. I don't see things getting better any time soon. You and I, as individuals, can only do so much. We need to focus on people interested in honest dialogue and not let hatred pollute our lives. People should listen more to each other and less to the pundits in their government offices, removed from the reality of the street. More than Vietnam, it's the pressing issue of today. And I'm glad you want to know the reality."

Nothing he mentioned surprised me and hearing it spelled out was helpful. But as the landscape continued to shift in one direction then another, it deprived me of a lasting sense of security.

When the walls in Bobby's small apartment started closing in on us, he would walk me through the streets of the city. One jaunt took us over the Hill, across the Boston Common, and down Columbus Avenue to Dartmouth Street. Prostitution flourished at a club called 411 on Columbus. I wanted to go in, but Bobby convinced me I would be throwing my money away. "Being young and White, they'll charge double, or triple. And you could walk out of there with more than a smile."

He saw the puzzled look on my face.

"The clap!"

I couldn't have been happier exploring the city with Bobby, especially in the lesser-known parts of Boston—the South End and Bay Village. Our conversation could be so engaging that the world around us faded away. Other times, we viewed the city as a stage, everyone playing their role—the hippie chicks with flowers in their hair selling incense, businessmen running to their next meeting, mothers wheeling babies in the park, and the all-too-familiar guys selling "spare" joints. My role was to observe and learn.

On our side of the Hill, many people our age were in the anti-war movement. Over on Columbus Avenue was another type of protest, the Student Nonviolent Coordinating Committee (SNCC). I asked if Flower Power and Equal Rights had the same objective. "They don't always see eye-to-eye, but they're both pushing for a better society," Bobby said. It occurred to me that I was better informed about the Civil Rights Movement than the anti-war campaign. Neither hippie nor Black, I existed between the two, searching for self-identity.

On our way back to Anderson Street, Bobby's voice slowly drew me out of my preoccupation with a very short mini-skirt, "You express your thoughts well. Have you always found it easy?" He asked.

I laughed, "No, man, I never can say exactly how I feel."

"Artists, writers, and musicians spend their whole life figuring out how to do that. The rest of us, well, some do better than others. Part of it is the willingness to reveal who you think you are. You want to understand, along with being understood. Which is more important?" he asked.

"Both! To be aware of what's goin' on around me and within me, then to be able to express myself more clearly," I said. "To understand and to be understood are two sides of the same coin, don't you think?"

"Someone must have stressed to you the importance of communicating clearly," he wondered.

"It was my mother, especially in high school. She knew how difficult those years were and would insist, 'Just say what's bothering you; get it off your chest. I promise you'll feel better.'

Rodney was another who encouraged me, 'Don't be afraid to ask if you don't understand; next time, you won't need to pretend.' And now you, Bobby. Showing no fear to be yourself is inspiring."

He looked down with an unfamiliar face. A long silence followed. What had I touched on? Without a word, we continued walking. By the time we reached the apartment, his old self had returned. But whatever I stirred up remained a mystery, raising the question of how well we know anybody—or ourselves.

Few could escape the division in the country—politically, economically, and racially. Conservatives viewed the changes in society as irresponsible, fashionable, and motivated by sexual promiscuity. Liberals wanted more diversity and felt it was time to rectify social injustices and strive for greater equality for women and Blacks. In 1965, the unemployment gap between Black males was 2.5 times higher than for White males. The average middle-class Black family had $6,600 in accumulated wealth compared to $70,700 for middle-class White households. For African Americans, segregation and poverty had created a destructive environment that was unknown to most White Americans. Whites didn't acknowledge what Blacks clearly understood: how deeply White society was involved in the ghetto. White institutions created it, White institutions maintained it, and White society condoned it.

Each of us managed these stresses differently. Arthur found relief driving his Thunderbird down Boston's Storrow Drive at break-neck speeds; Steve seduced as many women as possible, Dos drank too much, while Bobby and I listened to Coltrane until the birds came home. And laughter! There was plenty of laughter with Arthur and Bobby going through their antics. We kept the demon of discord shut out in the cold, with no room for it in the small living room on Anderson Street. Back in the dorm, alone, without music or frivolity, my mood could descend into worry, and I'd fret about race relations. The news was either dominated by wishful thinking about the Vietnam War or the reporting of another White cop shooting a Black man. The instability in the country compounded my sense of vulnerability. I anxiously watched to see which way the country and my friends were drifting.

In December, Leigh decided to return to England after breaking up with Vickie. Before leaving he said, "I want to give you a parting gift of sorts. I meant to introduce you to Katy and Carol, who live across the street. They were part of the Cohasset scene, where I met Vickie."

"Yeah, man. I would dig meeting a woman."

At 11 Anderson Street, where they lived, Leigh made the introductions. Both were unattached and hot, but Carol immediately caught my fancy. Her light brown shoulder-length hair, pretty smile, and slender figure spoke to me loud and clear. I struck up a conversation with her as Leigh and Katy talked about Cohasset. Carol must have found something interesting about me because her body language was enticing. Good thing too, since my ability to woo a woman left plenty to be desired. She suggested going out for a walk, probably to avoid her roommate's watchful eye. We strolled along the Esplanade next to the Charles River at sunset. Her hair glistened in the fading light. I nervously chatted about electronic school and my friends across the street.

"I've seen you going in and out of 16, glad we finally met," she said.

That's encouraging, I thought. She's noticed me.

On the way back, I held her hand and the sensation was electric. Part of my mind raced forward to a promising evening, but the present was too exciting to blow on a fantasy. With a coquettish smile at her doorstep, she said, "You're coming in, aren't you?"

Man, this woman is forward, I thought. This could be really good. In my zeal, I nearly fell over, opening the door for her. Katy and Leigh were still in the living room discussing his departure and hardly noticed us. Carol and I sat at the kitchen table, drinking coffee and trying to carry on a coherent conversation until the anticipation became too much for both of us. She reached over, took my hand, and led me toward her bedroom. The fantasy became a reality. But wait—my teenage terrors of pregnancy burst the bubble. In high school, a girl in the junior class became pregnant and left school in disgrace. We all knew who the father was. What kind of life could either have, saddled with a baby before finishing high school? Not an unusual story for the early '60s, but it put the fear in me. No babies, please. Even if I'd had a chance to have sex in high school, I would have been too terrified to function.

"Carol, I should run down to Phillips Drug Store." She kept moving toward the bedroom, saying it wasn't necessary. Ahh, the PILL! Her first kiss said, "I'm experienced."

After discovering each other thoroughly, we lay side by side in silence, enjoying the afterglow. This evening had been extraordinary, and I wanted to turn it into something more than a one-night stand. Carol asked what I was thinking.

"You're amazing; I've never known anyone like you."

Summoning up the courage to be as open as possible, I confessed to not having much knowledge of love-making. She grabbed me and whispered, "Don't worry, I'll teach you."

I relaxed into the pillow, reveling in my good fortune that extended well beyond this apartment. Carol was moved to confess she was in and out of therapy. No big deal; many people were either seeing a shrink or self-medicating. I welcomed her honesty and filed the information away. Later, I pondered just what her struggles were. She didn't appear unhinged, at least no more so than most people who were dealing with the chaos of the times. I'd watch for signs, otherwise enjoy her company. Within half a block on Anderson Street was my personal triad of education: learning a worthwhile trade in electronics on one corner, being tutored in the mysteries of women on another, and navigating my way into the world of jazz and Black culture on the third. Of the three, jazz and Black culture had the deepest impact. Jobs and women may come and go, but what I was learning from Bobby, Arthur and Steve continued to form my outlook on life.

Meanwhile, Steve, a humble man with modest aspirations who showed little interest in the hippie scene, asked about my LSD trip.

"A positive and profound experience," I told him, "but not for everyone."

My failure to elaborate only increased his interest.

"Would I dig it? How long does it last? How did you feel afterward?"

"Look, man, without knowing the quality on the street these days, it's hard to predict. Why are you interested in LSD?" I asked.

"Lately, I've been thinking I'm too mainstream. Too young for the middle of the road, I need to branch out and see what all these hippies are doing. Right?"

"You think I'm a hippie?"

"Hell, no. With your button-down shirts and trimmed hair, you ain't no hippie. But don't you think they're into a whole different groove, looking for more than what money can buy?" Steve asked, looking across the street to the wasted real estate.

"Maybe some are for real, but too many have just jumped on the bandwagon, protesting while living on trust funds. I hope I'm wrong, but if you look closer, there aren't many poor or blue-collar kids trippin'."

I can dig it. Still, I feel I might be missing out. Hippies aren't prejudiced, either. Maybe someone should turn on LBJ, then the war would stop," Steve joked.

"You're not the first to think of that."

"Do you think I might freak?" Steve wondered.

"No. The ones who freak have no self identity or a screw loose. You're cool. If you decide, I can cop on the Hill. You want me to drop with you?"

"Damn straight! You think I'm trippin' out here alone? Hell no!"

This behavior was out of character for Steve, a new side to him that I admired. And he was right; now was the time to stretch out beyond the safety net. None of us identified with the hippie movement, but since this was the mid-sixties, everyone felt the optimism.

During the week, Steve said, "Go ahead and cop."

Late one Saturday night, when everyone else in his house was asleep, we popped the purple pill. Chops was there. He showed no interest in joining us on our trip, but wanted to witness what could be a bizarre scene. Steve and I lifted off slowly. Chops kept insisting on hearing Coltrane's "Impressions." With no response, he started to sing the head to "Impressions."

"Give it a rest," Steve barked. "This is not the time for Trane."

Chops couldn't even get us interested in smoking a joint.

Fed up, he split, saying, "Later for you crazies."

The acid wasn't strong, but as the warp and weft of the norm unraveled, Steve let himself morph into another state of being without a trace of fear. He looked the same, talked the same, yet he said his angle of vision had shifted and widened. I was impressed. For me, this was a pale version of my first trip.

In the wee small hours, he announced it was time to tour a "typical ghetto household." Under normal circumstances, Steve could be hilarious, and with the added effect of LSD, he had me in tears. We crept past the grunts and snores of the sleeping family on the second floor down to the entryway.

My tour guide pointed out the lack of furniture. "In the ghettoe, you keep nothing important in eyesight from the front door, don't want passers-by to get any ideas of breaking in."

Too high for comments, I nodded. In the dining room, there was a large table without a single chair or sideboard. Under the influence of LSD, one expects the unexpected, but this was surreal.

"You might ask, why no chairs?" Steve noted. "In this house, you don't sit and linger over your food."

"Why not?"

"Because the roaches come out in droves, and you have to beat 'em back with a stick," he said, trying to keep a straight face.

"Roaches?"

"Oh yes, we even have pet roaches. There goes Betty Sue up the wall now." He burst into muffled laughter.

In my present condition, it was hard to tell whether there were roaches or not. After considering all the ramifications of a dining table with no chairs, we moved on to the kitchen.

Steve drew my attention to the distinctive patina on the walls, ceiling, and stove. Years of greasy fried food had left its mark. Only the most basic utensils were available to aid in the culinary process. LSD can make your stomach uneasy; the sight of this kitchen didn't help. I suggested heading back upstairs.

Steve's tour had me in stitches, but what was beneath all his laughter?

Was he so easygoing that these conditions weren't an embarrassment?

Most likely he was saying, "Look at this. What an excuse for a functioning household!" His "tour" raised a number of questions about how he honestly felt. But being stoned on acid wasn't the right time.

Back in the penthouse, silence fell over us as Coltrane's "Spiritual" played. After a few pokes on a joint, I settled on the couch to sleep.

Months later, Steve confirmed the lasting effects of his trip. Not the hallucinations, but a shift in perception. "I'm more comfortable in my skin," he told me.

CHAPTER 5

BIGOTRY IN COPLEY SQUARE

Now that Leigh had returned to England, all my companions were Black except for Carol. Finding acceptance within a minority community gave me a lot to consider. Everyone I'd met so far had become a friend. What was the attraction, other than jazz? The first possibility to pop up was our shared sense of being "outsiders." It's not a stretch to believe that most Blacks feel outside mainstream America. Some may see that as good, while others want in but are denied full entry. My failure to be included in the mainstream was in a different universe. Nevertheless, we shared alienation. I began seeing their world-view more clearly than mine, probably because their opinions were fully formed, whereas mine were in the make. When I'd first met Rodney, I found his way of communicating easy to follow; the same on Anderson Street, despite my naivete. But why were they interested in me? Being White was no novelty, but maybe my attempt at honesty appealed to them.

Wandering through Boston's Public Garden one day, Bobby and I sat to watch the swan boats paddle by; children waved to couples on the bridge, all very genteel. Without much forethought, I told Bobby, "I wish I was streetwise like you guys—if I'd grown up in your neighborhood…"

He laughed. "I doubt Roxbury would have treated you better than the country. Be grateful for growing up in clean, open spaces, free from school gangs or brutal policing. And not everyone is so lucky to have a cabin to retreat to. I could've used a hip place to escape the bullshit during the long hot summer."

Then I wanted to know about the impact of racism on him. "Do you remember the first racial insult thrown at you?" As soon as the words left my mouth, I wanted to retract them for fear of embarrassing him. *One of these days, I'm going to push too far,* I thought.

Without hesitation, he began, "At an early age, maybe five or six, a few White kids in the neighborhood said I was darker than them. No real harm; I probably called them a snowflake or pale face." Pausing, he gazed over the pond, then nodded and turned directly at me as if to say, "This one still hurts."

He started with a subdued tone, "When I was ten, on my way to a doctor in Copley Square, an Irish cop went out of his way to stop me. 'Why don't you niggas stay in Roxbury where you belong?' he taunted me."

Bobby straightened up, took a deep breath, and again looked right at me, saying, "That hurt. It wasn't the "nigga" so much, hardly the first time I'd been reminded of being a nigger. No, what cut me was the idea that I belonged in only one place, denied even the possibility of venturing out to see what was around the corner or over the hill. I wanted to run back home and hide in my bedroom."

"What did your parents say when you told them?"

"A few days later, I told my older brother, not my parents. My mother, you'd like her, would have burst into tears. My brother wanted to find the son of a bitch and kick him in the balls."

As he talked, I couldn't respond with anything more meaningful than, "What a miserable motherfucker! What's with these Irish cops?" I remembered Rodney's grandmother had warned him about them as well.

"Irish, whatever. *White* is the issue. Back then, they were all White and mean. As I grew older, I found ways to beat back such ignorance: 'Fuck the Man, I'll go wherever I damn well please. Black is Beautiful, and so am I.' That attitude didn't come of its own accord and didn't always work; self-loathing persisted. It's part of being Black in White America; we're looked at as less than human, certainly less than White. With all the discrimination in housing, education, and employment, it doesn't exactly build self confidence. Rejection embeds a lasting impression: 'They all hate me; I must deserve it.'"

I expected to hear a heavy story, but this was more than I'd bargained for. Bobby broke the pregnant silence with, "My story is no different from that of most Black Americans in one way or another. Ask Arthur or Dos, and see what they say. It's a run-of-the-mill story for my people."

His experience illustrated that I, a White man, could never understand what it means to be Black. All I could do was not perpetuate the cycle. The walk back to his place was silent, lost in the heart-wrenching story. I sank into the couch. Bobby asked what was with the long face.

"My head is still struggling with what you just told me. I can't digest such cruelty. It leaves me feeling alienated."

"Alienated? Why alienated?"

Rubbing my forehead, I said, "Because my life has been so different. If we are the sum of our past experiences, how can I fit into your world? Your childhood story reinforces that I'm from another country."

Bobby turned on the stereo. "Let's hear some Trane. He always makes me feel better. You shouldn't be down; diversity is good. Otherwise, how could we learn from each other? Attempting to understand a world different from what you know will bring pain and joy. Most Whites fear what's behind our Black faces, knowing the history, knowing damn well they don't want to be Black in this country. You aren't afraid, are you?"

"Not exactly, but maybe out of my depth. Fear *is* there." I shouldn't have said that, but I wanted to be on the level with him; he didn't appear to be holding back. Then why should I?

"Afraid of what?" he asked.

I should have known where my fears came from, but I didn't. Certainly, being unsure of myself and shame played their part. The more I learned about the plight of Blacks, the more guilt-ridden I felt. As I began to speak, I watched for a reaction, a signal to continue or shut up.

"I fear losing what I've found. You guys might disappear. With the country so divided, what if we can't hang out anymore?"

Bobby nodded his head with a distant look, probably visualizing the revolution. But then he grimaced, saying, "Don't worry, my man, you're solid with us."

I needed to hear that. But not knowing how to respond, I moved the subject along. "I thought I moved to the Hill to learn electronics, but the major course is right here in this room. A lot about Black life in America goes over my head, but the music… Thanks to you, I have a growing appreciation for its power and beauty."

"Yes indeed, listen to the truth in the music and…"

I interrupted, "I have to ask, how can anyone explain away what that cop said to you?"

"I'm not sure I can, but the Black Muslims explain it by seeing all Whites as devils."

This is what I get for asking these questions: Whites are the devil! And Black Muslims? My equilibrium was so easily shaken.

"Black Muslims?" I parroted.

"The Nation of Islam—a big subject on which I'm no expert. We can talk more about them—Malcolm X and Muhammad Ali—another time. But now let's kick back, listen to Trane."

The music played but failed to drive out the images of Black Muslims wearing red fezzes and toting rifles, roaming the streets looking for White devils to eradicate. Then Coltrane's solo on "Out of this World" grabbed hold of my ear and lifted me to the place where social discord didn't exist.

What good fortune to have a friend who trusted me with such a personal trauma and I wanted to make sure the afternoon ended on a positive note. "I wasn't all that together before I met you" I told him. "Everything changed when I walked through your door. You took me in like a long-lost brother, you hipped me to both the music and what's happening in this country. Getting to know you, my jazz guru, has changed my life."

Bobby laughed. "Jazz guru, huh? That's a first."

As I got up to leave, he stopped me and said, "Gerard, both of us know a place where racism is rendered null and void, where all is bright and clear, where all are welcome to have shared and individual experiences at the same time."

Descending the stairs to the street, I thought about how cruel people can be to each other, individually, communally, and nationally. Racism is a prime example, but there are too many other examples to think about. His story angered me, but I had no idea where to direct it.

The slave traders, both African and European?

Our lame government, who condoned it?

White people?

Myself?

Walking up the hill to my dorm, Bobby's phrase, "my people," popped into my head. When was the last time I heard a White person use that phrase? Sure, I felt a link to the freaks on the street and might say, "my kind of people,"—but not *my* people. When he said it, Bobby referred to all Blacks in America, who came here in chains, stripped of their language and religion, and sold off as property. In White America, we had no such unifying event. We are divided between gender, religion, politics, and economic success. Even regional differences—the Northeast versus West Coast—keep Whites separated. If White people said "my people," they would be referring to an organization, a communal trait, or people they work with, but never would they mean all Whites in America. The camaraderie between African-Americans—brother this, sister that—was what I missed. No, how do you miss what you've never had? That's what I was looking for. I'd never be a "brother," but I stood with them.

On my bed, I stared up at the cracks in the ceiling where faces started to form as I considered Bobby's explanation of why Whites fear Blacks. I could easily relate. Having a Black man as a best friend brings up problems not found within our own race. But I didn't mind. If there was a hidden agenda—mine, Bobby's, or anybody's—now was the time to disclose it. From their side, I honestly couldn't see what was in it for them. For me, there was much to gain, primarily inclusion. They were all more informed and sophisticated. Their culture felt rich where mine was lacking, at least to me. New England country ways are rooted in the British "reserve." That never worked for me, and thanks to my mother's Midwestern influence, I knew I didn't need to conform. I wondered if all Blacks were more expressive.

The self expression inherent in jazz was what attracted me over other forms of music. Bobby's enthusiasm to seek out the last bit of marrow in a new Coltrane piece may have been unique, yet all my Black friends could spontaneously enjoy the moment. WASPs acted as if it was against God's Will to enjoy themselves. I concluded there was no cause for alarm even though I couldn't see what attracted them to me.

On a fresh autumn day, Bobby and I walked over to the Fenway Victory Garden allotments—a community garden of over 500 plots that had been established in 1942. Standing on the pudding stone bridge over the Muddy River, we watched the ducks below. Even as the chit chat flowed, questions and doubts from the large reservoir in my anxiety-fueled mind bubbled up. I told him I worried about always being in his apartment when his friends came over.

Annoyed, he raised his hands like a preacher about to deliver fire and brimstone, "That's a lame thing to say. Are you uptight when people come by? You don't act it. You're not the first honky they've seen." With less intensity, he continued, "Race shouldn't be a barrier to friendship; at least not for us. If someone comes over with an attitude, don't plug into their negativity. Don't let what we have be affected by narrow-minded people. Our thing is about respect and trust, not skin color, right?"

I muttered, "I hope so."

"It's true, some militant will try to mess with your head. There's a lot of anger out there, but dig, the heart and soul ain't got no color."

"No shit."

"I must admit," Bobby continued, "the first time you came up and expressed an interest in jazz, I wondered if you were being straight. Then you told your Coltrane story, and even though you didn't get the music, you dug his presence. A man among men, you said. Only a true seeker would speak in such terms, convincing me you were who you appeared to be, and nothing has changed my mind since. Now that we've cleared that up, I want to ask you how does being the only White boy in the room feel?"

My reactions were as changeable as New England weather; I had no simple answer. I stalled by beginning with my background. "You know I didn't have a multiracial experience in central New Hampshire. With little choice of friends, the family up the road had to do. But those early years were fine."

Better move it along before you put him to sleep, I thought.

"I was never good at sports. When I started to become interested in jazz in grade school, no one took notice. In high school, my hope for finding like-minded friends faded into 'just friendly will do.' My classmates thought it odd that I was not interested in the Top 40. Naturally, we didn't have any racial problems. How could we with only one lonely Black guy, sent up from Washington, DC? He tried his best to be White. Who could blame him? Good looking, excellent in academics and sports, yet when he asked a girl to the junior prom, the truth about our 'liberal and open-minded' parents surfaced: 'Not with my daughter!'"

Bobby gazed off into the ozone. I broke his spell, saying, "My captivating story could put an insomniac to sleep, right?"

"Sorry, I tripped out there momentarily imagining you in the country. That's a long way from Deckard Street in the Berry, where I grew up. Ghetto or country, we all have shit to put up with. But we both escaped and ended up on Anderson Street."

Bobby laughed, "Now ain't that some bizarre shit?"

"Bizarre hardly covers it; more like destiny, I'd say. I came to the city full of hope to find a way into the world of jazz and people I could relate to. When our paths crossed, I realized the gods had dealt me a winning hand."

"Now I'll answer your question," I continued, "about being the only White guy in the room. If the conversation is heated over abuse from cops or the system in general, I am uncomfortable until I remind myself the comments aren't necessarily directed at me. It's not easy to hear your reality, but I want to understand. Most of all, I'm just happy to hang out with you."

"That's cool," Bobby said.

I took this opportunity to voice my nagging concern over the imbalance in our relationship. "Shouldn't there be a more equal give and take between us? I'm doing all the taking and not giving much."

Turning to face me, Bobby declared, "You ain't no freeloader. You share yourself, and what's more important than that? Arthur might know more about politics, and I have a larger collection of jazz records, but these aren't what friendships are based on. You're doin' just fine with the brothers from the Berry."

We both laughed. I looked up at the sky turning pink while the ducks continued to splash around. I hadn't said all I wanted, but I rarely did.

Bobby had a knack for deciphering my stunted chatter and gave a big smile. On the way back, we passed two homeless drunks asking for a handout. Surprisingly, Bobby gave them money. My predictable reaction was, what a waste, they'll just spend it on drink. Because of my brother's alcoholism, I had issues around drunks.

Then out of nowhere, Bobby dropped a one-liner that felt like cold water thrown in my face: "What separates them from us is as fragile as the ash on your cigarette."

My head reeled at the notion that in a blink of an eye it could be me living from hand to mouth. But he was right—I should be more grateful for all my good fortune.

After I thanked Bobby for another great walk, I went to see Carol. Occasionally I stayed with her on the weekend, but I didn't make it a habit. If she wasn't depressed or anxious, Carol had the remarkable capacity to listen, then calmly respond. A perfect counterbalance to my constant vacillating between exhilaration and being left in the dust by fast-talkers across the street.

I began to unwind at the sight of her smile. Reflected sunlight filled the room as pianist Bill Evans' "Peace Piece" played on the stereo. We sank into the sofa covered with the essential Indian spread.

Carol took pride in her appearance; she was never seen with unkempt hair or in a housecoat, even on weekends. Today, she wore a clingy blouse and short skirt, and the relaxed atmosphere helped me voice the tangled emotions bouncing around in my head. She'd heard much of it before, so I cut my monologue short.

She played the devil's advocate, "If you're overwhelmed, take a break, back away from the intensity." We both knew that wouldn't happen, so she continued. "You have a strong attraction to Bobby and his world, right? So are you willing to do the work to keep up?"

I was puzzled by how insightful Carol could be with my issues, yet thrown by what appeared to me as minor disturbances in her own life. If she was down, I had to pay attention, careful not to light her short fuse. But tonight all was well and we went out for dinner.

CHAPTER 6

THE CLUBHOUSE

Since Bobby and Toni had only moved into her apartment on Anderson Street just two weeks before I showed up, there were few visitors at first. But that changed quickly and it soon became *the* place to hang out. Initially Toni didn't mind, but we sorely tested her good nature. Steve and I would come knocking as soon as classes at NIT wound up. Bobby was usually there, recuperating after a long day of installing central AC in the new Government Center buildings. Arthur split his time equally between BU and Bobby's; Dos and others also filtered through. I couldn't imagine a better scene with all the music, conversation, and the shared joint. By the time Toni came home, the grass and food were usually long gone. When she asked for a smoke, everyone looked the way Sylvester the cat did with Tweety Bird in his mouth. We'd split, leaving Bobby to face her frustration. We knew if our behavior continued, Toni would give us the boot, Bobby included. But we kept coming back anyway.

Toni was part of a Motown-style group called The Indigos. The other members would come over to Toni's to prepare for a gig. One time, Paul, the bass player, came in looking clean and sharp. He quietly disappeared into the tiny bedroom to change. Emerging with a new outfit, he strutted around, looking for approval. Disappointed, he went back into the bedroom. In no time, he re-emerged in new threads. Still not satisfied, he tried yet another. To my amazement, this continued until he received the desired result: "Oh yeah, now we're talkin'. Sharp, Paul." The final touch was a scarf—but which one? I expected Rod Serling to walk through the door, smoking his cigarette, saying, "You've just entered the Twilight Zone." Such emphasis on fashion was beyond me.

Maybe it was a "Black thing."

One of the many unforgettable evenings at the clubhouse started like any other: music, chatter, and reefer filling the air. Rodney, who I'd introduced to Bobby, had made one of his rare appearances with Paula Larke, an up-and-coming singer in the Richie Havens style. They'd hardly sat down when someone put on Chico Hamilton's "Conquistador." Paula and Rodney jumped to their feet as if on cue and started to dance. Mesmerized by their fluidity, entirely in sync with the music and each other, I was convinced they had worked out the moves in advance. Not a dancer myself, I was overly impressed, but everyone else dug it too. As the music came to an end, the dancers resolved most gracefully.

Silence followed until the room erupted: "All right!" "Right on, yeah, man!"

Later, I asked Rodney how long they had rehearsed.

With a shrug, he said, "No, man, we just felt the music, wanted to dance. I only see Paula at the Unicorn (a folk music club on Boylston Street)."

"Really? But you at least knew the music, right?"

"I don't remember hearing it before—maybe," he said dismissively. "Great tune, don't you think?"

I don't remember how Lionel "Lucky" Francis entered our lives, but he was a force to contend with. Speculation arose that his luck had run out in Harlem and he'd come to Boston to explore new opportunities. His physical appearance was nothing special. But his personality and demeanor were another story. With the gift of gab, Lucky fancied himself as a charismatic street hustler. Given a chance, he could talk the bark off a tree. Trouble was that his facts rarely added up. Always scheming to achieve the fame and fortune he so rightly deserved, no one could trust a word he said, but we all liked him. Listening to his latest ploy to achieve stardom, or at least money, was more entertaining than going to the movies.

One of Lucky's attributes I envied was that he could pick up women as easily as breathing. On our way to the Esplanade one sunny afternoon, I challenged him to get a date in the next ten minutes. He didn't even need *that* long! *His* challenge was keeping a woman longer than a week or two.

Not a great jazz fan but afraid to miss out, Lucky tagged along with us to the Jazz Workshop to hear Chico Hamilton's band. During the break, Lucky told us that Chico would be coming to Anderson Street after the last set. Likely story!

Lucky had more stories than Walt Disney. But this time he proved us wrong. Chico and a few other musicians came over and stayed until early morning. I'd never been in the presence of anyone so hip. Miles Davis was definitely cool, but Chico's demeanor was more street—the way his body moved in rhythm with his speech. A sharp suit complimented his curly hair and mustache. With the dimly-lit smoke-filled room, slick banter between the musicians, and Lucky being Lucky on steroids, the evening should have been filmed: "After Hours on Anderson Street." I was happy to hang back and take mental notes. This was a vision straight from my daydreams back in the cabin. I'd made the scene.

While waiting for his dentist, Dos flicked through the *Boston Globe*. To his astonishment, there was an interview with Coltrane in the paper. Dos blurted out to all in earshot, "Dig this. Trane's in the paper!"

The next day, Dos brought the article over to Bobby's. None of us were news junkies. The only news we read was in underground papers, so Dos' attempt to grab our attention fell on deaf ears.

"I found this article in the newspaper…"

"Paper? What newspaper?"

"What the fuck—?"

But when Dos announced, "No, man, wait! It's *Coll-traane*," the room fell silent.

With the reverence generally reserved for a Sunday preacher, Dos read, "My music is a spiritual expression of what I am. I want to point out to people the Divine in a musical language that transcends words. I want to speak to their souls."

Bobby was the first to jump up, arms flailing, dancing, and laughing. "He does! He does! He speaks to my soul. Coltrane's a preacher on the saxophone."

Bobby hastily put Coltrane's *Live at Birdland* on the turntable as I commented, "I guess I knew that, but it's wonderful to hear Coltrane say something—*anything*—about his music."

"I don't know about the Divine," Arthur reflected. "But he's certainly saying something on *Olé*."

"I knew y'all could dig it," Dos said, bobbing his head from side to side, eyes twinkling.

Later, Bobby and I picked up the conversation that had been started by Coltrane's comment. Bobby insisted, "Coltrane is self-conscious…aware of a Higher Power. A few of the 'New Thing' musicians are headed in the same direction, expressing not only what is, but what could be. That music is a model of the universe and possibly a direct link to the cosmos."

The cosmos? I'm into Trane's music, I thought, *but he lost me on that one.*

"When the music is really happening, is that the *cosmos*?" I asked. "It's a force in my life, but…?"

"I don't know, call it the heavens, infinity, or the void…the name makes no difference," Bobby said. "The point is, we travel outside, no *inside* ourselves, to experience a greater reality than our everyday existence. Labels aren't important, going there is. As Jackie McLean says, "*One Step Beyond.*"

My jazz guru had raised the ante to a new level—music and metaphysics.

Miles came to town, this time at the legendary club Lennie's on the Turnpike, located along Route 1 in Peabody, ten miles from Boston. Peabody was not as convenient as the Workshop, and now that Arthur had upgraded his ride to a Corvette and Dos was unreliable, how would we all get out there? Then it struck me, I could borrow my Dad's station wagon. I would hitchhike up to my parents on Friday night, drive the car back to Boston on Saturday, then load everyone in for the ride to Lennie's. I'd have all day Sunday to return the car and hitch back to Boston. Dad went along with the idea, knowing I would not drink and drive. Good thing he didn't say, "no smoking pot and driving!"

Arriving early at Lennie's was essential to grab the front row, center table. The club was nothing to boast about. The musicians were sandwiched between the claustrophobic stage and the low acoustic-tiled ceiling, with just enough height for the upright bass. Flimsy curtains, originally red, now the color of nicotine, concealed the two windows behind the stage. The surrounding walls were peppered with album covers. A fake beam ran down the middle of the ceiling in an attempt to create a country atmosphere. Being a country boy, I knew better. Did anyone else notice or care? We weren't out for cocktails and a meal; we were there to hear what Miles, or at least his band, had to say.

Miles being Miles, he'd only play the head, then ease over to the bar to chat with any available woman (there were usually plenty), before returning in time to finish the tune. This was normal for Miles; we expected nothing different. Besides, the rest of the band was so heavy we hardly missed Miles. His drummer Tony Williams, a local, meant his crew was there in force, egging him on. Wayne Shorter, on tenor, was never a disappointment. To the contrary, he tore the place up. As Miles once said about him, "He knows how to scramble those eggs!" Pianist Herbie Hancock and bassist Ron Carter completed the band—the classic quintet!

Those in the audience who were deeply connected to the music could recognize a musical reference and respond immediately. They were in the groove. I was always a step or two behind—oh yeah, now I get it! My fallback reaction was: *It's another Black thing.*

When I talked to Bobby about it, he merely said, "Listen with more concentration, then you'll be right there with the musicians, not just following each note but anticipating them."

I had doubts, but listening to Miles' band that night, I could predict the next drum roll or cluster from the piano. Thank you, jazz guru!

Later that summer, Miles brought Joe Henderson (tenor) and Bobby Hutcherson (vibes) with him to Lennie's. This was the first time I'd seen either one of them. Wayne must have been unavailable; old Joe had a beautiful tone, but not Wayne's fire. Bobby Hutcherson was familiar from Jackie McLean's *One Step Beyond* and his new release *Happenings*, featuring the haunting song "Bouquet." The unusual cover, shocking pink, featured a gorgeous woman with a determined look. Many discussions focused on what she was conveying—other than her overt beauty.

Hutcherson struck me as one of us. He gave off an approachable vibe, personally and in his music. I could imagine him hanging out with us on Anderson Street. Only a few years older, he came on the scene just as we began going to clubs and buying records. Playing in Miles' band was a one-time event for him. How lucky we were to be there!

On the ride back to Boston, Dos questioned why Miles had such an attitude and Bobby Hutcherson didn't.

Bobby responded, "Jazz musicians tend to be loners with their bands always in flux. Have you ever heard of a group of jazz musicians going to the park together, having a picnic the way cops or sports teams do? These guys live and create on the edge of society. A few are famous; many are notorious because of their bad choices. Some develop behaviors to protect themselves: hipness, sophistication, addiction, or in Miles' case, disdain. Lord knows, with all that has happened to Miles—you know about the police beating him bloody in front of Birdland, where he was playing in '59? Shit, who wouldn't cop an attitude? But some say his hard-ass persona was a cover-up for being shy. His sound does have a vulnerable quality, *Jazz Track* is a perfect example; so heartfelt."

Bobby's preference for the avant-garde emerged as our listening sessions continued.

"Just listen and see what you think," he encouraged.

The Ornette Coleman Trio at the "Golden Circle" Stockholm was the first. I failed to find a hook into Ornette's music. Bobby must have known and didn't bother to turn the LP over.

"Any thoughts?" he asked.

"I like the drums."

"What is it about the drums you like?"

"The cymbals, they sound unusual." I said.

"Ah, that's because he's playing oversized cymbals. What about the horn player?"

"He doesn't appeal to me."

"What's not appealing?"

By this time, I had confidence in expressing an adverse reaction without fear of sounding square. "I guess Ornette's tone and phrasing sounds unfamiliar, jerky."

Bobby nodded. "You're not the first person to say that."

Without further discussion, another musician from the avant-garde went on the turntable. Albert Ayler was a strong tenor player, but I didn't warm up to him either. Yet I instinctively knew that some day both he and Ornette would become an essential part of my record collection. Bobby used Coltrane's *Ascension* to introduce me to the promising young musicians that Trane had assembled for the recording. Hardly easy listening with the beat mostly implied, yet with repeated listening it grew to be a favorite, opening the way to the avant-garde for me.

During our next session, Bobby unexpectedly played a few pieces of gospel by the Staple Singers. I was shocked how the lead singer took the song "out," the same way tenor sax player Archie Shepp could do on a simple tune. I'd never considered a connection between gospel and free jazz before.

"You think Trane and some others have been listening to gospel?" I asked.

"The way I hear gospel," Bobby said, "it's less about religion and more about release. Letting go of the centuries of pain and misery. In free jazz, the music is less about a melody or rhythm and more about self-expression. Coltrane and Archie Shepp approach their music that way, and what about Cecil Taylor pounding away on the piano as if it was a drum set?"

Max Roach's album, *We Insist, Freedom Now Suite,* was featured next. Bobby asked for my opinion. The music was wonderful, but the social commentary dominated. When Abbey Lincoln sang, I found her lyrics about slavery deeply disturbing. Bobby wanted to know more.

"The song 'Driva' Man' is so heavy. The image of the boss man whipping them to work harder is unbearable. I guess the world is no stranger to such depravity, past and present, but when it's in your face, well, I wonder."

"Wonder what?" Bobby asked.

"How blind we are to the evil we do. Listening to Abbey Lincoln sing 'Ain't but two things on my mind, driva' man and quittin' time' made me wonder how this country can ever come together with our horrendous past?"

With a grimace, Bobby sighed, "Realistically, not all at once. The Native Americans say, 'Walk a mile in my shoes, then speak.' We all need to become more conscious of others and their humanity. You and I are doing that, seeing people as individuals, not by race or class."

I sat back, watching him talk, his hands and face communicating more than words. My apprehension around the subject dissipated with his caring remarks, opening my heart. A surge of affection for Bobby welled up, nearly bringing me to tears. I had no benchmark for such strong emotion for a man. No surprise that what followed was fear rising up from wherever it hides, ceasing any further introspection.

Bobby continued talking while I plotted my exit without revealing my near freakout over my own feelings. I avoided eye contact and looked out the window momentarily, knowing how easily he saw through me. I muttered, "Today's session gave me more to digest than just music. Sorry for my angst over Abbey's song. Your advice was just what I needed to hear. I'll catch you tomorrow,"as I walked out the door.

Was I elated or terrified by these intense feelings? Both. My relationship with Rodney came to mind. Rodney's support and encouragement to self-analyze was a gift from the gods. The relationship faded, but what I'd gained didn't. Right from the start, my connection with Bobby proved to be more profound, covering music, culture, emotional support and expanding my circle of friends. He quickly became my best friend and advocate, guiding me into the ever-expanding vista of the music and self.

Did I love him?

If I did, what was stressing me out? Was it *gay* to love another man? The mere possibility alarmed me. My reaction wasn't rational or about Bobby; the anxiety was my inability to appreciate love in whatever form it came. Maybe most twenty-year-olds would react the same way. Arthur, Steve and Dos didn't seem so vulnerable, although they could be better at hiding their emotions with fast talk. And love—what did I know about it? As a teen, I had an overwhelming crush on a girl, but that wasn't love. I resolved that my phobia would *not* affect my relationship with Bobby and I would stop letting fear dictate my life.

I was walking down the hill to the convenience store, Bobby noticed me and threw open the window of his third-floor apartment to yell down. He shouted something about Coltrane just as the window pane came crashing out of its frame, slashing his arm. Fortunately, Mass General Hospital was only a block away.

Stitched up, we hustled back.

"I just bought Trane's new release, *Kulu Se Mama,*" Bobby said, "and waited to hear it with you."

"You waited to hear it with me?"

The prophetic photograph on the album cover, Coltrane playing his tenor with a mystical light on his forehead and horn, hinted at its unique contents. When the first few notes from the title track filled the air, Bobby's freak accident was long forgotten; we were off on a new journey. The inclusion of Pharoah Sanders and an additional bass and drummer added another level of energy. The group gently started the title track with drum rolls and conga, then a vocalist chanted the theme, all quite rhythmical. When Pharoah and Trane entered, they snapped us to attention. Playing with such strength and authority, Pharoah groaned and growled while Trane wove in and out of Pharoah's incantations. Unable to contain himself, Bobby shrieked with joy. While the conga player kept the beat, the two tenors created a distant African landscape.

The room hummed long after the needle lifted off the LP. Both of us hesitated to speak, reluctant to break the spell. Bobby and I had been blessed by the preacher on his horn, his sermon was more in tune with my psyche than words could ever be. When we eventually spoke, the comparison to Coltrane's *Ascension* came up. But there was no direct connection besides Pharoah on both recordings. Then Bobby laughed, "We want Trane to move in a straight line with his music, making it easier to follow him. But dig it, his spirit is too free for that. It's up to us to follow wherever he takes us."

CHAPTER 7

MALCOLM X, MUHAMMAD ALI, AND THE BLACK MUSLIMS

Bobby needed to see his mother so Arthur offered a ride. Since I'd never met Bobby's parents, I jumped in. They lived on the sunny side of Deckard Street in Roxbury, lined with well-maintained, three-story brick apartment buildings from the '30s. Bobby's mother opened the door of her ground-floor apartment with a huge smile. What else did Bobby inherit from her? She carried a few extra pounds, and her ample bosom strained the buttons on her blouse. The winged eyeglass frames looked dated compared to the rest of her otherwise fashionable appearance. She hugged her favorite son so passionately he struggled to breathe. Embarrassed, Bobby pried himself loose and went inside. Arthur received a less passionate greeting. She extended both hands to shake mine. "And who are you, dear?"

"Oh, just a White boy we picked up on the way over," Arthur laughed.

"Mind your manners, Arthur!" She reached to pull his ear, but he was too fast. Bobby told his mother I went to the trade school next to his apartment.

"It's so nice to meet your new friends from Beacon Hill," she said, motioning me to sit down, "My Bobby never has problems finding friends. Who would like coffee?"

After she left the room, Arthur mimicked, "*My Bobby...*" then snickered. Bobby grimaced. Obviously a loaded comment, but I missed it.

I began to take in Bobby's home. The living room was well-furnished with a matching sofa and side chairs, a TV in a cabinet, and a large picture window facing the street, covered with translucent sheers to let the sunshine in. Everything was so clean—the hardwood floor, the richly colored carpet—with not a crumb or cat hair in sight. A faint odor of furniture polish hung in the air. From what I could see of the kitchen, the appliances were new and spotless. Bobby had mentioned his father had a good job, and once the kids had left home, his mother worked part-time. His home was on a different planet compared to Steve's. *This wasn't the typical ghetto household*, I thought. *But maybe it was.* Roxbury was as diverse as any community, but I was slow to figure out the obvious.

Arthur and I drank coffee as Bobby disappeared into the kitchen with his mother. When he reemerged, Bobby wanted me to see his room. A large poster of Coltrane's *Blue Train* hung above the empty stereo cabinet adorned with carefully arranged knickknacks and a candle, Bobby's altar to the Master Musician. His devotion to Trane had a long history.

I was grateful for the chance to peep into Bobby's background, where love flourished. "Too bad your father isn't here; where is he?"

"Working. Next time."

His Mom waved as we motored away. Next stop, Jerome, better known as Romy, a childhood friend of Bobby's who lived just down the street.

"Who's Romy?"

"You'll see," they both said with a giggle.

After a persistent knock on his door, Romy cracked it open for a look. Recognizing Arthur and Bobby, he allowed them to squeeze through, then abruptly slammed the door shut. "No White folks allowed," read the invisible sign. Stunned, I asked myself, *Stay in the hall like a wimp or man up and knock? Even if this guy is a raving racist, Bobby and Arthur will protect me. Knock on the friggin' door!*

At that moment Bobby let me in. "Don't pay any attention to him," he whispered. "He'll try to mess with your head."

Inside, my jaw dropped. In the middle of the living room stood a high-powered rifle mounted on a tripod, aimed out to the street. This *was* messing with my head. Standing next to the rifle, fists waving, Romy proclaimed that violence was the only way to get White America's attention, refusing to look at me as he ranted.

I've been ignored before, but this was outright hostility. Looking for an escape, I diverted my view out the window. A young couple walked by; she wore fashionable bell bottoms, and he sported a newsboy cap—nothing special, but a safer place for my attention.

Hardly taking a breath, Romy continued his tirade, forecasting the coming revolution with quotes from H. Rap Brown and Stokely Carmichael. I'd heard the names in passing, but they meant nothing to me except possible trouble. Avoiding Romy's eyes, I finally took a seat and glanced around the room. The Black Power posters and slogans covering the walls compounded my jitters.

Because his captured audience, Bobby and Arthur, weren't responding as he expected, Romy turned up the volume: "The only politics in this country that's relevant to Black people today is the politics of revolution!"

His raised voice vibrated worse than a dentist's drill. If we didn't leave soon, my head was going to explode. For the life of me, I couldn't fathom why they brought me here. If it was a joke, I wasn't laughing. Under normal circumstances, being the only White in the room didn't bother me. But here I was ready to split as soon as I saw the rifle. Maybe they thought I needed to hear the militant perspective firsthand. A forewarning would have been appreciated.

Finally, when Bobby and Arthur got up to leave, giving each other the DAP (Dignity and Pride) handshakes, I glanced at another poster: "To understand White supremacy, we must dismiss the false notion that White people can give anybody freedom."

As soon as we hit the street, I demanded an explanation.

They both had sheepish expressions and admitted it was a set-up to see if I could maintain my cool in Romy's company *and* how Romy would react to me.

"Really? And what if he went off on me?"

"Come on, man! You think we'd sit by and let Romy jack you up?"

"Well, maybe not. And who are Rap Brown and Stoky Carmichael?"

"Stoky? Actually, it's *Stokely*. He and H. Rap Brown are Black activists," Arthur said. "Brown's done a lot of voter registration down South, so has Stokely. But he's better known for his involvement in SNCC (Student Nonviolent Coordination Committee)."

"Well, that's all very educational, but I could have done without it. That rifle was no joke either!"

"I didn't know he was armed," Bobby confessed. "He needs to go out more, get some fresh air. He lays up in his crib for days on end. Not healthy. In hindsight, Wig, it was a bad idea."

That night, sleep was impossible with Black militants marching through my head. Black Nationalism could spell trouble for interracial relationships, although none of my friends appeared interested in the militant arm of the movement. Nevertheless, I was desperate to voice my fears to Bobby.

In April 1967, Muhammad Ali's refusal to be drafted into the Army on moral grounds dominated the news, and his Heavyweight Championship title was revoked. Immediately, Ali became more respected by Black Americans and anti-war protesters. When he joined the Nation of Islam, the press had a field day, "CASSIUS JOINS HATE GROUP". (The irony of Whites complaining about a Black hate group wasn't lost on me). More people took a second look at the organization and its leader, Elijah Muhammad. I asked Bobby if now was the time to enlighten me on the Nation of Islam (NOI) and its founder.

"I'm no authority on the subject by any stretch," he began, "but I'll tell you what I've heard. The NOI is a positive force within the Black community, requiring men to clean up their act and take responsibility for their babies, get a job, pray, and treat their wife with respect. If you don't toe the line, the NOI comes down on you hard."

Bobby took a deep breath. "The controversy is around their leader, Elijah Muhammad, and his theory of the origin of the White race. The original Man, claimed Muhammad, was Black and pure. Then came an evil scientist who decided to kill all the dark-skinned newborns, allowing only the lightest-skin ones to live. Six hundred years later, this blue-eyed "devil race" of lying, cheating, murdering troublemakers was banished north to the hills of Europe, leaving behind the Black Empire in Africa.

Black Muslims literally believe that the White man is the devil. Easy to see how they could come to that conclusion, especially in America. Whites have been telling lies and lynching us ever since we set foot on this continent."

He paused to see if I was keeping up. "There's no denying that the behavior of too many Whites is evil, but a few are doin' the right thing. 'Course, they're not the ones in power. When I first heard Elijah's theory, I lost interest in looking further into the Nation—just too far out."

I'd heard enough and wanted to leave, but that was impossible in the middle of his discourse. Instead I sat hunched over, picking my fingernails, calculating how many African-Americans believed this ridiculous scenario. With the possible exception of Romy, nobody I knew took Elijah's message to heart. But then again, how could I know for sure? I wanted to believe they were sincere in accepting me. But I did know how precarious my situation was, floating down the river with each foot in separate boats; straddling the Black and White communities. How easily I could land in the water.

Bobby continued, "The NOI pressured the US government to hand over a state as reparation for all the years of slavery. Fat chance of that happening. And dig this, both the NOI and the KKK have something in common. They're against integration and mixed marriages."

With no comments forthcoming from me, Bobby decided to change the subject to Malcolm X. I'd heard of his assassination a year ago, but had no clue by whom or why. The press didn't make a big deal out of it; clearly, most Whites were glad to be rid of him.

Bobby's thumbnail sketch of the man went this way: "When Malcolm was a teenager, he moved to his sister's in Roxbury and took up the street life. At twenty, he was sentenced to ten years in the Charlestown Jail."

For what? I wondered, but the moment to ask was lost.

"Malcolm's older brother, a Black Muslim, finally turned Malcolm from the hustle to the NOI. After six years in the joint, Malcolm was released and became the minister of a mosque in Harlem. He and Elijah grew tight. But when Elijah sought help from the KKK to form a Black state, Malcolm started to lose respect for his leader."

"Elijah had allegedly fathered many illegitimate kids and his over-the-top lifestyle also alienated Malcolm. And dig it, when Malcolm went to Mecca and saw every race under the sun circling the Kaaba, he said 'later' to the devil race theory. I mean how could the devil enter Mecca? He left the NOI on his return, pissing off a whole lot of members. Retribution didn't take long, he was gunned down in February '65. Three NOI members were convicted, but within the community people knew that the real gunmen were protected by the cops and the FBI, who had feared Malcolm's growing popularity across racial lines. How Malcolm evolved from a street hustler to a Black nationalist to a human rights activist impressed me. And breaking with the NOI took courage," Bobby concluded.

Seeing my dazed look, he promised to continue Malcolm X's story another time.

CHAPTER 8

1967: LONG HOT SUMMER
OR SUMMER OF LOVE

The summer season started on June 2 with a protest by the *Mothers for Adequate Welfare* who were objecting to their measly payments. They chained the doors of the welfare offices on Blue Hill Avenue in Roxbury, and the moment the police arrived billy clubs started swinging. Arresting 44 demonstrators only made things worse. Blue Hill Avenue was shut down for three days.

The Summer of Love was in full swing. Hippies flocked to Haight Ashbury. Meanwhile, Americans watched troop movements in Vietnam on the nightly news, and Dr. King came out against the war. Massive anti-war rallies were held in New York City and Los Angeles, while Abbie Hoffman demonstrated against capitalism on Wall Street. Race riots erupted in Newark and Detroit.

The hippies spread optimism with "flower power" that summer. Their slogan, "Make love not war," sounded right on, and

I hoped to put it into practice. The time to act was now, before the winds of fate changed.

NIT shut down for the month of June, a perfect chance to get out of town and see what was happening on the West Coast. Steve wanted a break too. "The ghetto can wear you down, stepping over drunks and trash, looking out for the crazies and junkies. We could sit on the dock of the bay, right?" He admitted hitchhiking through middle America wasn't his idea of a good time though. "I'll join you in Frisco if I can scrape enough money together for a bus ticket."

Solo anything wasn't my style, but this trip felt right from the start. Hitchhikers littered the road, all heading to the same place. When a car stopped, before I could speak, the driver would say, "Yeah, I know—Frisco. Get in."

In upper New York State, a sedan stopped. A man rolled down the window, saying he was on his way to Chicago. Within an hour, we were fast friends. An art teacher from Goddard College in Vermont, he was anxious to see his wife, teaching at a theater camp south of Chicago. "Man, it's been three months since I took care of business. When I see her, I'm gonna make up for lost time."

He dug jazz—Miles, Trane, and Thelonious Monk. The hours flew by as he drove through the night. As we neared Chicago, he insisted I stay at the theater camp.

"Sure, but where can I sleep?"

"Don't you worry about that. There's plenty of women there looking for company."

We pulled into the camp in the afternoon, everyone looked hip. My new friend's wife was waiting, and both hung around just long enough to introduce me to a hot-looking woman. He told her I had been on the road for a long time, knew a lot about jazz and art, and would appreciate some company. I straightened up, lit a Lucky Strike, and tried to look the part. We wandered over to the cafeteria for a bite, but I was too nervous to eat. Conversely, she was entirely at ease, asking which jazz musicians I was into and what I hoped to find in San Francisco.

After a short stroll around the camp, she led me to her cabin. I thought this kind of affair only happened in movies or books. She wasn't the least bit shy. What a night! In the morning, I was relieved to see her next to me; it wasn't a dream. After breakfast, we wished each other farewell as I grabbed my backpack and strutted out of there as if I was a character in a Kerouac novel. It *was* the Summer of Love!

The two-thousand-mile trip from Chicago to Frisco went faster than I liked. One ride took me through the Rockies at night; I woke up in Utah. Two more rides, and I was in "The Haight." The neighborhood lived up to its reputation, with freaks everywhere. They knew I was a weekend hippie and tried to liberate me from my money and my small piece of hash.

"Hey man, this is the hippest cafe in the Haight. Come on in."

All the activities in Golden Gate Park reminded me of kids on recess, uninhibited, and having fun. The San Francisco Diggers, a community-based group of activists and street theater actors operating during 1966 to 1968 in the Haight-Ashbury neighborhood, ran a "Free Shop" near the park. The donated goods were freely handed out to whoever needed them. Such an unorthodox concept made me realize there was more to the hippie movement than long hair, bell bottoms, and psychedelic music.

Heading south on Route 1 to L.A. was a hitchhiker's dream; every car stopped. I spent one night on the beach at Half Moon Bay, the next amongst the redwoods in Big Sur. The following day, moving too fast down a beautiful stretch of Route 1, I asked to be dropped in the middle of nowhere. Sitting on a rock, I stretched out to embrace the blue sky meeting the sea-green ocean on the horizon, waves thundering below and gulls catching the updraft. For an hour, I needed nothing, and nothing needed me. Freedom! Never before had I experienced unbridled joy—alone. That moment made the entire journey worthwhile.

Back on the road, a VW bus stopped. The driver said he was going to the Valley northeast of Hollywood. "You want to crash at our place in the Valley? Stay as long as you like."

"Sounds great!"

"We're out during the day; you'll have to find your own groove. Is that cool?"

West Coast hippies were into a different head trip than the freaks in New England. Their friendliness and trust demonstrated again there was more going on than just sex, drugs, and rock 'n' roll. For a week, I sat in a treehouse and took long walks in the Valley, avoiding the tarantulas I'd been warned about.

On my way back east, I landed in Needles, California, near a railroad yard late at night. Ever since reading *On the Road*, I'd had a romantic fantasy about jumping a freight train. Now was my chance! But what about those yard men? They'll beat the shit out of anyone they catch.

Running across the freight yard, which was lit up like a football stadium, I threw my pack in an open boxcar, then barely managed to hoist myself in. I didn't care where the train was going, even back to L.A. With my heart pounding, the train started to pull out—slowly—very slowly, then stopped. Now what? Not yet out of the yard, voices came closer and closer. I could feel the blows of billy clubs that were sure to come any minute. Shit, they're right outside. What are they doing? Then the locomotive started to chug away, but I wasn't moving. The train lumbered off into the night, leaving my car disconnected in the yard. I couldn't believe it! Half an hour passed before I dared to climb down in disgust. Running from shadow to shadow, I escaped unscathed. Now with filthy clothes from my failed adventure, who would pick me up? A sign of an all-night gas station cast a bluish glow against the pitch-black sky. I could clean up there.

"Any chance I can sleep here?" I asked the young attendant.

"I wish I could let you, but they'll fire me," he said. Then, "Fuck it! If you want, hide under the desk. Not much space, but better than being outside; it gets cold."

At sunrise, I crawled out, feeling like a pretzel. Thanking my friendly attendant, I stepped out on the road again, looking wistfully back at the freight yard. What would Kerouac say about my feeble attempt to catch a freight?

On the long trip east, I anticipated my return to Anderson Street, eager to be with everyone again. This solo journey had given me time to wade through the backlog of my unresolved feelings about Bobby and where my place was in their community. The larger question of where in American society I belonged would have to wait. I felt grateful for the direction of my life and decided my affection for Bobby was of no concern. Goals for the future were out of focus, but as each ride brought me closer to Boston, they seemed unimportant. I wanted to go with the flow, see where it carried me. So far, life had been far beyond all expectations.

The boys at the clubhouse were curious about the West Coast scene and how I fared hitchhiking.

"Did any pervs pick you up? Any horny women?"

They all approved of the night at the theater camp, but my other adventures were less interesting. What did they know or care about hitchhiking? Within an hour, we were carrying on as if I'd never left.

When I asked about Toni, Bobby acknowledged she wasn't happy. "This is her crib; we need to include her more and be aware of her needs."

Arthur agreed to cut back on his sardonic comments, and I promised to stop acting as if I lived there. Bobby replied, "No, no, don't stop coming; we just have to cool out before she comes home."

I asked what else was going on with Toni.

"I wish I knew. Probably the same shit as most of us. I don't think it's about me, but I haven't been paying attention. A few weeks ago, we took LSD. That seemed to open doors for her."

"And what about *your* acid trip?" I asked.

"Oh, I had a blast. Listening to music was deep. Didn't you mention seeing music on acid? During our trip, Toni and I connected, really connected, but it didn't last. Now she acts disappointed with just about everything except her singing. That's going better than ever. We should all go down to the Sugar Shack to hear her with the Indigos soon."

Out of the blue, Arthur asked if I planned to stay in the dorm in the fall or would I be interested in finding a place together.

"Do you need to ask? When do we start looking?" I replied.

"Let's wait and see, we have time. Just wanted to know if you were open to the idea."

Dos was on board, but Bobby wanted to avoid facing the possibility of leaving Toni.

Coincidentally, when I went to see Carol, she mentioned returning to Baltimore until September. "You know I've been anxious and depressed lately, so I decided to have a few months of therapy back home. You want to crash with me 'til I leave? And can you stay 'til I return, help Katy with the rent?"

The invitation didn't need repeating. I jumped at the chance to be with her *and* to hook up my stereo. Shacking up across the street from Bobby's and within steps of NIT, I had it made in the shade.

On my next visit with my parents, I casually mentioned taking my stereo to Boston.

"Oh, it will now fit in your dorm room?" my mother inquired.

"I'm moving in with Carol and her roommate until September. Then I hope…"

My liberal mother went berserk, pointing a finger at me, "I'm not paying for your school so that you can shack up with some woman!"

For once, I didn't take the bait. "That's cool, I can handle it from now on," was my level-headed response.

The only reaction from my father was a grunt as he walked out of the room. He hated confrontation.

I went to see my old employer in the dry goods section of Boston, behind Jordan Marsh, for a part-time job. He must have had a soft spot for me.

"When you're free, just come and punch in."

My classes and overhead were minimal; this job plus bussing tables for Scotty at the Sheraton Hotel in the Back Bay on the weekend, would cover my expenses. I first met Scotty when I was coming to Boston with my father. He was a regular on Coffee Corner. After I moved to the city, I scored grass from him occasionally but he didn't have much free time to hang out. Married with a baby can do that. When I mentioned looking for a part-time job, he said I could bus tables for him.

Despite her fragile state, once I moved in Carol seemed happy to have me around. I accommodated in every way: laundry, dishes, sweeping, and lovemaking. When she wanted to talk, I listened—a reversal of our norm. In the back of the apartment, her bedroom was an irregular five-sided room with posters on the drab yellow walls, a worn-out floor, and a window that opened to a large air shaft. A light bulb covered with a scarf hung from the ceiling casting a soft glow over the sparse furnishings—a chest of drawers, a mattress on the floor with milk crates for end tables. And it was *hot*, but we didn't mind.

In the heat one night, we enthusiastically made love. Afterward, I lay drenched in sweat, Carol's head on my shoulder. Echoing voices from the air shaft drifted through the window on the heavy air. Unable to distinguish between the many conversations, they became a backdrop to this romantic moment. Looking up at the scarf-covered light bulb and the muted light glistening on Carol's face, for an instant, the ordinary became extraordinary. I remembered long, lonely nights in the cabin when I'd dreamed of this very scene, right down to the red scarf, but especially, a woman resting on my shoulder.

One of our listening sessions featured pianist Carla Bley. Bobby and I wondered why so few women were into jazz as musicians or in the audience. Just then, Gloria, a large amiable woman with a pecan complexion, came in wearing a flowing skirt and a brocade vest. One of the only women we knew who shared a similar passion for the music, she stood in the middle of the room surveying the situation, then laughed. Her jovial laugh rivaled Bobby's.

"Anyone want to go to the Newport Jazz Festival? Nina Simone will be there."

"Newport? Out 'a sight! But where to crash?"

She'd rented a small cottage in town for a month. "There's plenty of floor to sleep on if you can dig it."

Steve leaned over and whispered, "We won't have to crash on no floor. I got it covered." One of his many girlfriends was renting a motel room for the festival.

"Sounds nice and cozy, and just where do I hang my hat?"

"Wigman, come on! You think I'd leave you out in the cold? There will be room, but you don't mind if I take care of business, do ya?"

"That'll be very instructive, I'm sure."

"That's right! Learn from the master."

On Friday afternoon, Steve and I caught a ride to Newport from a regular on Anderson Street. He drove a not-safe-at-any-speed Corvair, equipped with an eight-track player and only two tapes—something by the Bee Gees (vetoed) and Charles Lloyd's *Forest Flower*, which played all the way to Newport continuously. I didn't want to hear it again for months.

The sun had set when we were dropped off at the motel.

Steve knocked on the door as I hung back. His "girlfriend" looked surprised to see him. Not a good sign. Only a few words were exchanged before the door was decisively slammed shut. As we walked away, I couldn't resist, "Typical!" Through the years, Steve had acquired a second nickname, "Steve the Stiff," and for good reason. He was notorious for coming up short or not at all. But he had a miraculous way of cajoling you out of your anger and turning the whole mess into a joke.

Without further comment, we plodded off in the dark to search for Gloria's little cottage. After numerous inquiries, we found her rental tucked behind two other buildings.

She greeted us with a smile and a plate of food and suggested we stake our turf before the hordes arrived. Upstairs, in a room the size of a handkerchief, we spread out our blankets.

Steve asked if I was still pissed. "No, man, we made it. This is going to be memorable, I know it."

We looked down the stairs in the morning to see the floor covered with bodies. All the regulars from Anderson Street, as well as new faces.

Bobby had taken charge in the kitchen, cooking up a mountain of hot grits and scrambled eggs as Gloria served. He was in great form, laughing and carrying on as he stirred the food.

We sat in the warm sun, filling our stomachs, then passed a joint around to aid digestion. Lounging on the miniature lawn, we easily forgot why we were in Newport, but Gloria herded us out toward the festival with a short detour to the beach. For once, I wasn't the only White person in the room. This mixed crowd raised my hopes that people could still hang out together, undeterred by the social upheaval. The breeze off the water carried the fragrance of optimism. If only I could bottle it for the future.

Lack of funds and too many joints meant we attended only two performances. That afternoon we caught The Herbie Mann Group with a special guest, Olatunji. The performance was good but Olatunji was a welcome addition to Herbie's so-so flute playing. In the evening, we returned for Nina Simone, the big draw for the day. Nina's behavior on stage was well known; if her audience weren't giving their full attention, she would walk off. End of the concert. Not the case that evening. She belted out six songs, saving the powerful "Four Women" for ending her show.

After Nina's performance, some returned to Gloria's for the night; others went back to the city. Too energized to sit still, Bobby, Steve, and I walked around the neighborhood. The conversation centered around Nina's song, "Four Women."

Bobby and Steve knew women of varying shades mentioned in the lyrics, while I was hard-pressed to think of even four women *I* knew of any shade. It didn't matter. We were like-minded in our love of the music and each other. The atmosphere was heady, as if the planets had lined up to allow this unforgettable day of music, tight friends, and a tangible sense of belonging. All was perfect in my world. It wouldn't last, but for now, I treasured the moment. Gloria's generosity made the weekend a resounding success.

CHAPTER 9

THE CLUBHOUSE

Bobby featured Thelonious Monk's *In Action* with Johnny Griffin on tenor for one of our listening sessions. While the record played, Bobby recalled a quote from Griffin: "In my opinion, I'm not from this planet. I'm only here paying off my dues for something I did wrong. I can't be from this place, there's no love here, and I love people. That's what is wrong with the Earth, no love, only hate. I'm a total misfit here."

This comment started a long conversation about why there was so much hate and so little love in the world. Viewing society through the smeared lens of racism and fear of changing the status quo explained a lot.

"But why is it easier to hate than to love?" Bobby asked.

I looked away, hiding my fear of intimacy.

"Fight or flight reflexes are more accessible than love, must be the way we're wired," I added, justifying my reactions.

"Yeah, you're right. You know I get more love from Trane than I ever did in church," Bobby admitted. "Religion works for many folks, but not for me. Did you go to church? Did religion water the plant of love when you were a child? And now is that plant watered and healthy?"

"My mother showed her love for us kids," I said. "My Dad loved us too, no question, but being a typical New Englander, he found it difficult to express his feelings." I looked for the courage to continue, "And now? I'm not sure. But I agree with you; Coltrane's music can take me toward peace and love." Casting my gaze downward, I said slowly, "To be honest, I've never been so close to anybody. My feelings for you are pretty intense. I don't know if that's love, but I am so fortunate you came into my life."

Bobby lit brighter than a Christmas tree, then gave one of his raucous laughs that filled the room. "I knew we could be close, trust each other. You're a brother from a different mother, and I love ya too."

Surprisingly, I didn't freak when I heard Bobby say he loved me. But I could sense myself reacting in the same way as my father would. Hesitating to respond, I questioned what Bobby meant by love. His intellect, knowledge of music, and open mind were what had initially attracted me, but now it was more than that. I felt something coming from the heart—a deeper emotional connection. I wondered if he was talking about the same thing? As uncertainty clouded my vision, I convinced myself that he hadn't meant love, that he'd meant something more comparable to admiration, respect, or appreciation. I took a deep breath and relaxed knowing I had only my intense attachment to cope with.

The room was now undeniably different. A layer of what isolated us had been peeled away. Just as fog burns off in the morning sunshine, I could see Bobby more clearly and, in his reflection, deeper into myself.

On a random afternoon, wandering through the South End with Bobby, I noticed a poster of a Black fist. He peeped my card—my uptight reaction.

"Does that poster bother you? It's about Black Pride, and it's *supposed* to be confrontational. But only toward the motha' fucks who keep us down." Bobby raised his eyebrows. "Black Power is about living your life without Whitey telling us what we can and can't do. If the Black community united across the country, then the playing field might become more level, increasing our odds. Whitey sure as hell ain't going to say, 'Okay boys, you're all welcome, may the best man win.' As in most cases, you can only deal from a position of strength."

After a long pause, Bobby added with a silly grin, "Since it's the dawning of the age of Aquarius, maybe the hippies with their flower power will turn all this negative shit around."

Ignoring his humor, I kept to the subject. "Level the playing field? Even with a united front, the Black population is too small to force the establishment to the table. So how do you get Whites to share privilege? Do you ever see that happening? Boston mayoral candidate Louise Day Hicks' supporters have made it clear they ain't givin' up shit. Bussing Blacks to South Boston? Not if she had won the election."

We sat down on a stoop and Bobby continued, "Privilege is huge, but there's more to it than that. As I see it, White America must acknowledge the truth about slavery. They have to face up to the bullshit lie: *Slavery wasn't really that bad, Blacks didn't mind 'cause the bosses were kind, and niggas were lazy.* The lie is a whitewash for what happened on those slave ships—families broken up, women raped, men flogged—the whole barbaric tradition. The lie pulls a white sheet over the rotting corpse of how America was built on the backs of slaves."

My ears were ringing. My brain receded into itself. Usually I had more stamina to listen to Bobby's views on America. But rotting corpses? My insides felt as if I'd swallowed broken glass.

Bobby saw my jaws getting tight and said no more.

To escape the intensity of the moment, I focused on the flow of young and old passing by. Nobody took the slightest notice of us.

He must have read my mind. "Let me say one more thing about race and that's it for today. We sit here, soaking up the sun, taking up space, but no one sees us. You dug it, too, didn't you? That's what it's like being Black—you're not important enough to be noticed. And if someone does notice, you're just a nigga. For a moment, sitting on this stoop with me, you're just another nigga."

I nodded in agreement, not knowing what to say. We lifted ourselves off the stoop, straightened up, and continued our walk. I had more questions, but white sheets over rotting corpses still flooded my mind.

Eventually I said, "When I saw that poster, it triggered feelings I'm not usually conscious of—guilt, sorrow, anger. Certain pieces of music have a similar effect. Ultimately, it's good to understand what's behind our reactions, right? But what we learn about ourselves can be painful."

For a moment, Bobby wore the same expression that had puzzled me once before, as if I'd touched on a raw nerve. He slowly nodded, looking away before saying, "Well, we just have to do our best and try to deal with what comes up, even if it's... well, you know, some heavy shit."

What was he talking about? I wondered.

He paused for a reset then continued, "I remember how strongly you reacted to the Max Roach record. Is that what you're talking about?"

"Yes, the guilt and shit."

"But anger, at who?" he asked.

"Anger at those responsible for all that brutality. Because of a few money-grubbing SOBs, so many had to suffer. 'Driva' Man' blew my mind, as well as Coltrane's 'Alabama' and Nina Simone's 'Mississippi Goddam.' I'm struggling to accept a history I never looked at before. I'm amazed that any African-American can trust a White person to give him the correct time of day."

We walked back without going further into what we can learn from watching the way we react to external forces.

CHAPTER 10

THE END OF AN ERA

On July 17, 1967, the radio blared out the unimaginable. Coltrane had died suddenly at the age of 40. I rushed to Bobby's as soon as I finished work, knowing he would be hysterical. He paced back and forth, tears running down his face. "Coltrane was too young. He had so much more to give. What is my life without his inspiration?"

Comforting him was impossible. The floodgates had opened releasing such a torrent of anguish that I suspected he was grieving for more than just Coltrane. I went into the kitchen and sat down to face my own sorrow. Looking back into the living room, I watched Bobby acting out his misery, strangely envious that he was so in touch with his feelings. Too often, my knee-jerk reaction was to hold back, unable to let go with both hands. Only the music could overpower my caution, releasing me to glide untethered. To see Bobby cupping his face in tears broke my heart. Then I tried to envision a world without Coltrane and couldn't. I opened the fridge only to see the depressing white glare of an empty icebox.

Toni arrived, hugged Bobby, and stroked his forehead. Sweet words had little effect; he couldn't hear anything but his tormented heart. There was no point in staying. I went across the street to Carol's. As I stared out the window into the grimy airshaft, my mind flipped from worrying about Bobby to my own despair.

A few days later, sitting around Bobby's during the Coltrane memorial marathon on WBUR, the announcer mentioned that *Olé* was coming up next. With Arthur's Vette parked right outside, everyone had the same idea: drive down Storrow Drive with *Olé* blasting, top down, and pedal to the metal. I was the lucky one to jump in first. No cop in sight, we flew alongside the Charles River, *Olé* filling the air.

Over the next few weeks, Bobby and I re-examined Coltrane's legacy repeatedly, looking for anything we'd missed. We took a fresh look at *A Love Supreme.* Not our favorite, but we realized the fullness of the music by reading the enclosed poem dedicated to the Supreme. Coltrane's life and work would take years to be fully appreciated. His death meant much more than the loss of a jazz musician.

As the country was being pulled apart by the Vietnam War, racial tensions on the street, and the chasm between the hippies and the right wing, Coltrane's music and life had great appeal across all classes, all nations, and all faiths. Coltrane's personal resurrection from heroin addiction inspired countless junkies to get straight. His dedication and devotion to the Higher Power triggered many to seek a spiritual path. Now, all of a sudden, jazz had a hollow sound. No one could ever fill the void left by this monumental man. There was only one Trane, and he had just pulled out of the station for the last time.

Knowing that Ornette Coleman and Cecil Taylor would keep the avant-garde moving forward gave little solace. Younger musicians, like Pharoah Sanders, Archie Shepp, and Marion Brown, gave promise, but this was no consolation for Bobby. His grief was out of proportion and it worried me.

Ever since Arthur had mentioned the possibility of our moving in together in September, I'd been counting on it. I could avoid the confines of the dorm and live with my close friends. Since apartments were too small on the Hill, we would have to look elsewhere. Then out of the blue, Chops mentioned that he was moving to Anderson Street. I asked what had prompted the relocation.

"Well, I'll be doing my service at Mass General Hospital."

"Service? What service? What did I miss?"

"Alternative service to the military." Patiently, he recounted his ordeal with the draft board. He received notice to report to South Boston for an induction exam a month earlier. Refusing to step forward when his name was called, he hoped his defiance would disqualify him. Nevertheless, he received a 1A classification. The following day, he applied for a hearing to contest his ranking.

A week later, armed with nothing more than determination, he entered the hearing room to face the board of five White, middle-aged men. One board member flicked through his papers, then asked Chops if he was afraid of fighting.

"I'll fight, sure I'll fight if someone threatens me, my family, or even this country. Damn straight, I'll fight. But not in a war that has nothin' to do with me or *my* people. Why should I go halfway around the world to kill someone who hasn't done a damn thing to me and only wants the same thing I do? Freedom. My fight's right here—on home turf."

Another interviewer made the mistake of calling Chops: "boy." That did it.

"You got my papers in front of you. Look, I'm 21. I ain't no boy, and I sure as hell ain't *your* boy!"

He was granted "conscientious objector" status that day. He chose to fill his two-year obligation to the government by working at Mass General as an orderly.

"That's why I'm moving to the Hill!" he said proudly.

This was routine behavior from Chops—wading through the bureaucratic maze of the US draft board without any fanfare.

"Why didn't you mention this before?" I asked.

"I'm telling you now, ain't I? Now let's hear some Art Blakey. You know what Blakey used to say?"

"No, but I'm sure you will tell us."

"At a minimum, jazz blows the dust of the day away."

On July 23, Detroit boiled over into what became a devastating riot. The news on the radio, the hot stuffy air in the apartment, the tension between Bobby and Toni, not to mention the loss of our hero, weighed heavily on everyone.

Arthur suggested going to see Rahsaan Roland Kirk at the Workshop. Months had passed since our last visit; Rahsaan would do us all a world of good. How can you be depressed after watching a blind man play three saxophones at once?

Bobby couldn't seem to catch a break. His job was reduced to part-time, but that was nothing compared to Toni's decision to move out in the middle of August leaving him a nearly empty apartment and no forwarding address. Bobby had seen this coming, but it didn't lessen the blow. Why hadn't he made more effort to save the relationship?

"Coltrane," he said unconvincingly.

After great lengths, Bobby discovered that Toni was living outside Kenmore Square. He asked me to go with him to visit her. I should have known better. Toni begrudgingly let us in, and as the conversation quickly deteriorated, I left.

In the midst of this drama, Carol returned from her emotional tune up. As soon as she opened the door, her renewed self confidence lit up the room. Wearing a thin cotton dress that was so short it left little to my imagination, Carol's entrance stopped my conversation with Steve in mid sentence. He smiled and said, "Later, m'man."

Equally excited to see each other, we disappeared into the bedroom to catch up. When she heard about Bobby's situation, she advised me to keep the dialogue positive and not to indulge him with pity: "If he continues to slide into depression, be careful not to get caught in the downdraft."

She agreed that my idea of living with Bobby could be helpful, but how did I feel about it? I assured her I was eager to move in with Bobby, Arthur, and Dos.

Furthermore, there was no possibility of staying with her since she and Katy were about to rent a smaller place on Phillips Street. Neither of us toyed with the idea of living together. Seeing each other when it suited us worked just fine.

Dos played up the advantages of living together to Bobby. "Dig it, between the four of us, we could afford a hip place. We'll scrounge up furniture. With Gee-rah's stereo and our two cars, what more would we need?" Bobby nodded with no enthusiasm.

Arthur did the upfront work, trudging all over Cambridge, looking at rentals. Then he read an ad for a new apartment building outside Central Square that could fit the bill and insisted I meet the agent, saying, "White's all right!"

On the first of September, Bobby, Arthur, Dos, and I would move to 10 Soden Street. The anticipation of living together was tempered by the end of an era. In just one year, I'd gone through such a transformation I hardly recognized myself. Most of the change had occurred in Bobby's apartment, and now that chapter had finished. But what I'd learned wasn't tied to any location; it was now part of me. Along with many other doors, the one to adulthood had opened at 16 Anderson Street.

The log cabin in New Hampshire

Rodney in Boston

Gary in the apartment on Fairfield Street

Leaving for the West Coast with Gary (left)

Beginning my long trip back from Malibu to be drafted

In my dorm room on Beacon Hill

Steve in his apartment in Roxbury

With Bobby in a photo booth

Arthur

Dos lighting up

Lucky

Hitchhiking to Haight Ashbury

With Carol in her apartment on Anderson Street

With Gloria, before going to the Newport Jazz Festival

The room I shared with Bobby on Soden Street in Cambridge

Passport photo, 1968

PART THREE

SODEN STREET

CHAPTER 11

LIVING LARGE

Just off Western Avenue in Cambridge, we rented a large 5th-floor apartment with an eat-in kitchen, a picture window that dominated the spacious living room, and two bedrooms! Arthur and Dos took the master bedroom, Bobby and I the smaller one, which had a touch of Haight-Ashbury: everything on the floor. Arthur found most of the furnishings while I contributed rugs and paintings from New Hampshire. The living room couch, arm's length from the stereo, sat directly across from a drip painting (Jackson Pollock style) done by my brother, David. It was perfect for studying while listening to extended solos from Trane or Shepp. We speculated at length on what, if any, was the connection between abstract art and the New Thing in jazz. Didn't Jackson Pollock's painting *White Light* on Ornette Colemans's *Free Jazz* album cover suggest there was?

The dynamics in the apartment were established within the first week. Dos, failing to find a bed, slept on the couch, his clothes heaped in the bedroom. Arthur had a similar system: one pile of clean clothes, the other dirty.

Bobby and I neatly stored our belongings in the closet. But he made little effort to make the room his own, which curbed my enthusiasm. I made excuses for his behavior, but Arthur and Dos didn't seem to notice. I gave Bobby space, hoping the new living arrangement would help him focus on the present. After I'd struggled to be emotionally open with him, his withdrawn behavior was disheartening. He moped around during the day and stayed out many nights. If there was a reconciliation between Toni and him, he failed to mention it.

Bobby's emotional problems brought back memories of my own bout with depression. The jolt of spending my days with discarded and forgotten patients who'd suffered too many electric shock treatments quickly led to a serious attitude adjustment. My release from the hospital was only a few months before I'd met Bobby, and he had become a major factor in my recovery. Why couldn't I do for him what he'd done for me?

No surprise, our streetwise friend Lucky came knocking before there was hardly a chair to sit on. He darted from room to room, commenting on what a hip apartment we had. Within the first week, one of his girlfriends called. "Is Lucky home?" I went off on him. Never without an explanation, he started in, "Well, well, I knew I'd be here, so I just gave her your number."

The '60s were filled with characters, and Lucky was undoubtedly one of them. Even with his jive shit, I took great pleasure watching him prance around the room, arms waving and finger pointing. His antics were often so entertaining we couldn't focus on what was being said.

Lucky's overactive imagination produced a continual flow of money-making schemes, although he knew better than to involve us. With his personable and persuasive character, I encouraged him to put his talents to good use—selling exotic cars or artwork. I failed to realize slick street hustlers never work day jobs.

"Yes, yes, what you don't know is, I'll be starting over at Peter Fuller Cadillac next week."

As much as I wanted to believe him, I knew there was about as much chance of that as finding a one-ended stick.

One evening, while sitting next to Lucky on the couch listening to Jackie McLean's *Destination Out* while Dos played the air saxophone, I noticed Lucky doing something peculiar with his eyes, sweeping them from side to side without moving his head.

"What are you doing?" I asked him.

"I'm practicing my 180."

Who but Lucky would think of such a thing? I guess a street hustler needs to keep track of who might be onto his game.

When all of us were going out for the evening, I had to pay special attention to ensure Lucky left the apartment. Usually the last one out, I checked the lights, burners, stereo, etc., then locked the door. If I looked down the corridor toward the elevator and didn't see Lucky, I knew he was hiding inside our apartment.

"All right, Lucky, let's go!"

"Well, well, I just had to use the bathroom, and…"

My roommates' friends weren't surprised to see me included in this new scene and often called me the "grayboy." It didn't sound offensive; in fact, I liked the term. I asked Arthur what it meant. "It just means a White person who isn't typically

White," he said. "You know, when the White is removed from your mindset."

Our combined record collection drew praise from our visitors. Bobby's contribution of mostly jazz made up the bulk; I added more jazz, Ray Charles, and a few Little Richard albums. Arthur and Dos filled in the Motown void—something for everybody. I noticed Chops, now a regular visitor after moving to the Hill, surreptitiously going through the collection and taking notes.

Looking over his shoulder, I asked, "What's shakin'?"

He quickly stood up, embarrassed. "Oh, just checking a few titles."

"Knock yourself out, there are some heavy tunes in there!"

"That's no lie! And dig it, on payday, I'll know what to cop. This collection is better than going to the library or some shit."

Bobby had been my most significant influence in jazz, setting the ball in motion. Now it was up to me to run with it. Soden Street was the perfect environment to do just that. Oscar Jackson played new and old classics on his WBUR radio show The Jazz Grotto. Other stations were playing jazz too, including a new FM progressive rock station, WBCN, that alternated between rock, soul, and jazz. WILD, the AM station out of Roxbury, played soul, Motown, and jazz. Even with all this, I missed my listening sessions with Bobby, now made impossible by all the activity and his fluctuating moods.

"You know who Ravi Shankar is?" Bobby asked one afternoon. "He's playing at the Music Hall on Mass Avenue." When I was in high school, David brought home an LP of Ravi's from his art school, High Mowing. Other than sounding exotic, I didn't give it much thought. Bobby's interest stemmed from Coltrane, of course. Trane's fascination for Eastern music and mysticism resulted in him developing a friendship with Ravi.

Trane had even named his recently born son after him. If Coltrane found something in Ravi's music, we needed to take a listen. Ravi Shankar was the perfect ambassador for introducing classical Hindustani music to the West, explaining basic concepts to a receptive audience. We both enjoyed the experience and compared the improvising section (alap) of the raga to jazz. Ragas are based on scales or modes, but also employ a specific formula for using them. Even though we didn't rush out to buy his records, a seed had been planted that would flower later in my life.

Living with fast-talkers meant my voice could be lost in the fray. The constant parade of fired-up "guests" only contributed to my predicament. To advance my thoughts beyond "in my opinion," I had to be explicit and convincing. Otherwise I'd be jumped on without mercy, told to sit down and get my shit together. There were debates on everything. Speculation abounded, with raised voices and stomping feet. As in politics, the presentation was of utmost importance. But if the content didn't hold up under scrutiny, your concepts didn't stand a chance. Consequently, my conversational skills improved rapidly.

This energy and enthusiasm did not migrate over to the emotional side of life. Talk about emotions could show vulnerability, and that was a problem with most males, Black or White. Bobby had been the one exception. He and I had always been able to talk in a way I found difficult with Arthur and impossible with Dos.

But now, between my classes, working after school, and Bobby's absence many nights, the closeness we once shared was fading. Any attempt I made to rekindle what we'd had was in vain. Even casual conversations between us were brief. Neither

Arthur nor Dos paid much attention; this was *my* problem. All I could do was wait for the fog of gloom to lift enough to better understand what was happening to him.

Carol's removed perspective was helpful, even if I didn't listen. She advised, "You're too close, can't see the forest for the trees."

"But I don't want to see the forest, I want my old friend back."

"That's not entirely up to you, Gerard. Bobby has to choose to change," Carol wisely pointed out.

Arthur and Dos talked about their cars so lovingly that I had to listen carefully to realize they weren't describing their girl-friends. When my stereotype of Black males and their rides surfaced, I wanted to deny the notion. Dos had a Dodge Fury equipped with a Hemi engine (425hp) and spring-loaded, four-speed shift. Arthur now drove a GTO (335hp). Between the two, there was enough horsepower to power a battleship. Bobby and I were only interested in getting a lift to the Jazz Workshop or up to Lennie's on the Turnpike (no need to hitchhike to New Hampshire anymore).

When I questioned Arthur about Black males and cars, he agreed there was a long-standing connection. "When cars became affordable and accessible to us, we hustled down to the nearest car dealer," he told me. "A vehicle meant no more riding in the back of the bus, no more segregated, filthy railroad cars. If the car was large enough, we could sleep in it, eliminating the pain of being refused a hotel room. It enabled us Black folk to get out of the South or the ghetto. We might not be able to afford fancy houses, but if we made enough money to be flash, we could drive a big, customized ride to impress. Speeding by a White driver can make my day. There's no denying I'm into cars—fast, pow-erful cars—always have. Is it a symbol? Could be."

On many Saturday nights, with no particular place to go, the four of us would speed off around the city. Roxbury, still largely unknown to me, was the most exciting, as my friends would entertain me with tales from their childhoods. Dos remembered the excitement of moving to Westminster Avenue, next door to his grade-school friend, Arthur. They were constantly in each other's houses.

When I asked why there was an abandoned synagogue on Seaver Street, Bobby said, "A large section of Roxbury was Jewish less than 20 years ago. There are still Jewish bakeries on Blue Hill Avenue, and not long ago, it was called Jew Hill Avenue." Before I could ask why the Jews left, the conversation changed to drag racing on Washington Street.

Always late with the rent, Dos had difficulty managing his money. He cautioned me, "If strangers knock on the door asking for Dos, he's not home and you don't know when he'll be back." The finance people were after his Plymouth Fury. Working a full-time job at the GE plant north of Boston in Lynn making parts for the B-1 bomber, his lack of cash made no sense. But when someone pounded on our door a week later, I suspected they were looking for Dos. I looked through the peephole to see two tough guys in the hall. *How did they enter the building without being buzzed in?* I wondered as they knocked again.

As I slowly began to crack the door, they forced it open. "Where's Dos? We're here for the Fury."

"I don't know where he is. I'd like to see him myself; he owes me rent."

They raised their eyebrows in disbelief.

One of them stuck out his chest to show the bulge of his pistol. "You tell that no count that we're on to him, and we *will* get the Fury."

When I recounted the incident to Dos later, he brushed it off with an unconcerned gesture. "Those guys are harmless; pay 'em no mind. I'll straighten it out with my next paycheck."

Dos successfully eluded the repo man by parking in a different spot every night. But one Saturday afternoon, he parked out front just long enough to run in. Within minutes, we heard the telltale sound of the Hemi engine starting up. That was the end of the Fury. It was a sad moment, and I sympathized with Dos; his car meant a great deal to him. His expression resembled a child who had been naughty, resulting in his toy being taken away. His cleanup: "No big deal, I'll get it back." I looked at Arthur, who shook his head without Dos seeing. "No way."

Dos still had a process (straightened hair) after moving to Soden Street, but he soon announced, "I'm going to shave my head and go natural." It didn't seem like a big deal to me, "do's" were yesterday's news. His mother had quite a different opinion. For lack of a better term, Dos' mother was a raving alcoholic with the emphasis on raving. When she called him during a drunken episode, Dos caught hell for whatever crossed her mind. The same way Steve had handled his living conditions on Highland Street, Dos turned these phone calls into a joke. He'd switch on the speakerphone and broadcast her rant to all until exhaustion overcame her.

Now she had a new bone to pick: She didn't approve of Dos' natural hair. This was nothing new; on my first visit to Dos' house, he drew my attention to the little doghouse hanging next to the back door. Of the three dogs, one for each child, Dos was permanently in the dog house. Everybody was grown and long gone, but in his mother's eyes, Dos belonged in the doghouse.

As we all laughed and made light of these phone calls, painful memories came up from my childhood. My brother David was a binge drinker even in high school. When his binges became more frequent, our family braced for his inevitable violent finale. Afterward, a period of weeks or months of sobriety and calm would follow. But as sure as the morning sunrise, the cycle would repeat. My poor parents had no means available to help him or themselves. Even as a child I could see David suffered the most, but I hated the effect his behavior had on our family. Ten years later, David found sobriety through AA and stayed sober for the rest of his life.

One evening, Dos came in carrying a new LP.

"What have you got?" I asked, looking at the unusual cover.

"Cannon-baaall," He replied, holding up the new Cannonball Adderley LP with a double image of him in a helicopter on the cover.

"Where did you find it?"

"Woolworth's, in the cut-out bin."

"Why this one?"

"Cuz it's got a *looong* track."

The title track, "74 Miles Away," was an instant hit. The "live" recording captured the dynamic interplay between the musicians and the audience, rarely caught on an LP.

The next day, Gloria dropped by.

"Check out this new Cannonball," we said as she planted herself on the couch. As the piece progressed, tension mounting, she began to bounce. When the piece went full throttle, shrieking with joy, she went airborne, landing on the floor, rolling with laughter. Just one of the countless times the music brought elation to those on Soden Street. Thank you, Woolworth's cut-out bin!

CHAPTER 12

ARCHIE SHEPP AT
KRESGE AUDITORIUM

The first musical event of the fall season was Archie Shepp's concert at MIT's Kresge Auditorium. We knew his music but had never seen a live performance, and his new band held great promise.

Wearing a brightly colored dashiki, Shepp burst on stage playing the tenor as if possessed. In quick succession, Roswell Rudd emerged from the other side, equally fired up on the trombone. Jimmy Garrison on bass and Beaver Harris on drums followed, increasing the velocity of the growing whirl-wind. No introduction. No theme. Just full-blown energy. As Archie commanded the stage, Roswell retreated to the back, commenting all the while. Building momentum, Roswell used his trombone as a battering ram to take the lead. Acting like a petulant child, Archie threw one-liners as he begrudg-ingly retreated. All this was warming up for the crescendo. Both taking center stage, sometimes dancing together and sometimes not, streams of pure passion flowed from their instruments.

Thanks to my jazz guru, I could let go and ride free on the cacophony of sound. How astonishing that four men could create a universe filled with the known and unknown. As the concert reached its conclusion, I felt let down because they had played for such a short time.

Bobby said, "No, they have been going for over an hour."

Convinced I'd be the first to leap out of my seat with applause, I joined the audience of 1,200, yelling: "Encore! Encore!"

Besides the music, I related to another aspect of the concert. The complexion of the band reflected my present world: Rudd (who was White) with three Blacks. As racial and political divisions in the country deepened, I found encouragement in watching this band work harmoniously.

Walking back to Soden Street, I thought, *If I went to an Italian opera without any idea of the story or knowledge of operatic singing, would I appreciate the music? Going with someone enlightened would help, but better still would be to accustom my ears to the genre beforehand. Through our listening sessions, I was ready for Shepp.*

"Because of you, my jazz guru," I told Bobby, "connecting to Shepp's music was as easy as floating downstream. No small thing!"

The music lifted the heaviness of Bobby's mood for the first time in months. Invigorated, we all sat around the apartment talking about the concert. After Steve caught the last bus home and Dos and Arthur went to sleep, Bobby and I settled down on our bed mats and continued philosophizing about the avant-garde and Archie Shepp. I wasn't about to waste Bobby's rebound on sleep. Again, we compared the abstract expressionist painters and the New Thing musicians. Both had moved beyond their constraining boundaries of representation or stated beat.

In this concert, Shepp showed his able chops to stretch the limits of tone and rhythm.

If Bobby had chosen to discuss the price of milk, I would have been equally fascinated. To see him smile and show enthusiasm moved me as much as the music we'd just heard.

He concluded by acknowledging how messed up he was. "I just can't seem to get past Toni. Something has to change, that's for damn sure. I haven't been much of a friend lately, and I'm sorry. Despite how I've been acting, I still love you."

I drifted off to sleep, believing Bobby was *back*. But underneath my optimism lurked an unsettling feeling that he had slipped from one mindset to another too easily.

Arthur and I were the first up the next morning. We ate our Cheerios in silence. Then he asked if I wanted to ride to his mother's house.

"In the Goat? Hell, yeah," I replied, referring to Arthur's GTO by it's popular nickname. Arthur's neighborhood had the air of prosperity with its large, elaborate Victorian houses. His childhood home stood proudly amongst them. His mother served us cold drinks in the parlor with its purple crushed-velvet sofa, matching side chairs, and heavy curtains, all deserving of this beautiful house, though I wished I could have opened the windows to remove the lingering smell of Spic and Span. I sat across from mother and obedient son, a sight to behold. To see your friends with their mothers can be revealing, showing a side usually concealed. In a soft voice, she asked how I knew Arthur.

"We met at Bobby's on Beacon Hill. "

"Oh, how sweet. Have you met Dos as well?"

"Yes, Ma'am, we all live together in Cambridge."

"Of course, you borrowed an old sofa, I remember."

Arthur was only three when his dad died, and his mother decided nothing would keep her from finishing college to become a librarian. Sitting there watching this slight woman, I wondered how she'd managed to be both a student and a mother. The prejudice she must have endured didn't show, at least not to me. My antenna, always sensitive to reverse discrimination, found none in this house.

They excused themselves to discuss selling and moving to a smaller house. Looking around again, I'd never seen a room so spotless, windows cleaned to the point where the glass disappeared, framed family photos on a bureau, a doily on the end table. Too bad Arthur didn't inherit his mother's sense of order. Staring out the bay window at Dos' house next door, I wondered how these mothers had raised children single-handedly. Dos' father had also died when he was young; Steve's and Chop's fathers were alive, but missing in action. Only Bobby's family stayed intact. Fathers leaving their children is another common stereotype of ghetto life. It may be true, but in the case of my friends, I couldn't see how it had adversely affected them.

The subject of fathers reminded me of when my dad stopped for a visit shortly after I'd first moved to Boston. He was in town to buy antiques and had come by for a chat. We sat on the stoop making comments as young women walked by, then he asked how I liked the city and my job (wrapping UPS packages for a dry goods company). Without hesitation, I told him I'd never been happier living in Boston. With a smile he said, "That's good." Later it dawned on me that he hadn't questioned how long I planned to wrap packages or what I would do with the rest of my life. He just wanted to hear I was happy without laying any expectations on me. How lucky I was to have such a father!

My reflection was interrupted when Arthur handed me a yearbook, saying, "We'll be a while longer, see who you recognize in here."

The usual suspects were easy to find. But seeing those phony senior-class photos, airbrushed to a paler version of reality, was embarrassing. Thank God, "Black is Beautiful" now! Arthur and his mother came back into the room to find me staring into space with his yearbook on my lap. "Doesn't Arthur look handsome in his class photo? Won't you have another cookie?"

If Steve's mother was the hippest, then Arthur's was the most regal and sweet.

Back in Cambridge, I told Bobby about meeting Arthur's mother and how I enjoyed seeing where they grew up. He had no response. What a difference in his mood from last night! He's tired, I told myself, but I knew better. As the days turned into weeks, I realized that night of the concert was a one-off, not a change. I faced the same dilemma. Should I do nothing, console him, or give him a swift kick in the ass?

No surprise that I began spending more time with Arthur. We were close, but in a very different way than I had been with Bobby. They were both intellectual, but Arthur was political, a womanizer, and consistent, while Bobby was spontaneous, emotional, and inconsistent. Arthur and I covered a different territory, more practical, not so much from the heart. But the change in my alliance came with guilt. I felt I had abandoned Bobby. Wait, he'd abandoned me! I resented his withdrawal and wanted to tell him, "Just get over it and let's move on."

CHAPTER 13

BACK FROM 'NAM

After sustaining critical injuries in Vietnam, my old room-mate Gary came to the US for R&R and dropped by for a visit. Even a blind man could see the war's effect on him—he was demanding, edgy, speaking in military jargon. Nearly dying in that ridiculous war (more absurd than most) had changed him. He showed irritation over my good luck in avoiding the military, then rebuked me for my anti-war attitude, saying I had no idea what was happening there. Gary wasn't exactly gung-ho, but he defended the US position. The conversation went no-where fast, so we took a walk.

Just up the street from my apartment, we sat on a bench in Central Square. Watching the motley crew of panhandlers, drunks, and hippies that Central Square tolerated, Gary blurted out, "Why are you hanging around with all those Black guys?"

He couldn't have said that, I told myself. I must have mis-heard. "Excuse me?" I replied.

"What's with living with Blacks?" he repeated.

"Because they're my friends," I snapped. This was too much for me. War casualty or not, I didn't need his attitude. I got up and walked away.

Annoyed to hear such a thoughtless remark, I assumed the army had polarized him. In high school he'd shown no evidence of bias, but back then I was too wrapped up in my dramas to notice his opinion on Blacks. He shipped back out to Vietnam without seeing me again.

Gary's visit reminded me of how narrowly I'd escaped going to Nam. How quickly I'd taken my good luck for granted. It could just as easily have been me on R&R, or worse, in a body bag. Then it struck me that while the draft was plucking every eligible young male, none of my five close friends had ever served.

Gary's "interest" in my choice of friends was still smarting a few weeks later when Scotty and Marie came over to check out our new pad. Since the summer, I'd been bussing tables for Scotty at the Sheraton Hotel, but we hadn't hung out in a long time. As we passed a "j" around, they commented on how together the apartment was, particularly my room with its posters of Frisco and Allen Ginsberg.

Then Scotty caught me off guard when he casually asked, "What's with hanging out with all the brothers?"

Was I in a recurring bad dream? I shook my head and responded, "Do you have a problem with it?"

"No, I don't. It just seems odd."

The atmosphere had been spoiled. How easily a thoughtless word can ruin everything. *The cut from the sword will heal in weeks, the cut from the tongue may never heal.* They picked up and left. I didn't see Scotty again until the following summer.

In contrast, my roommates' friends didn't mind a White boy in the room, at least to my knowledge. Other than Carol, Scotty and Gary were the only White friends I had. What was their problem? Scotty grew up in the multiethnic West End of Boston, and I didn't see him as the stereotypical bigot. But something unpleasant was lurking in both Scotty and Gary.

With these two incidents still rancoring, I asked Arthur for his *short* discourse on racism in America. Bobby had spent hours on the subject with me, but I wondered if he'd soft-pedaled the reality for my benefit. Another point of view could help me draw my own conclusions.

"Well," Arthur pushed up his glasses and thought for a moment. "A big subject, and I'll try not to ramble. In my opinion, there are two types of racism—individual and institutional. With individual racism, Whites, no matter how poor and desperate, need to know they ain't on the bottom. They want to be able to say, 'At least I'm better off than those niggas, ya know.' The scapegoat syndrome fits in here too—when the law needs a quick conviction, any nigger will do. This type of individual racism is a human condition—Whites don't have an exclusive on it, but they've learned to run with it. When a Black family moves into a White neighborhood and is stoned and routed out, they are also victims of individual racism, which many condemn—at least in words. Institutional racism keeps Black people stranded in dilapidated tenements, subject to the whims of slumlords, loan sharks, and red-lining real estate agents (denying a housing loan on the basis of race or ethnicity). And wait, let's not forget the fear factor: all Black men with their huge dicks want all them White women. Right?

"Racism is learned, passed down from generation to generation. Little kids don't know about skin color. Few stop to think, 'Why do I hate this man, this religion, or country? Why should

I be threatened by him, big dick or not?' People are sheep, don't figure shit out for themselves. The 'establishment' uses fear, very effectively, to lead the masses around by the nose in the direction of their choosing."

"Besides those big black dicks, what else has us White folks cowering in fear?" I asked.

Without a pause, he said, "Loss of privilege." He raised his eyebrows, waiting for a response.

I just nodded my head, knowing I took White privilege for granted.

Arthur's thumbnail sketch of racism should have been easier to hear by now, but it wasn't. I probably would always cringe when hearing the African-American version of this country's history.

As if I hadn't heard enough, I asked for more. "How can this ever change?"

The words rolled right off Arthur's tongue. "First, White people must acknowledge the brutality of slavery, the lynchings, beatings, and false imprisonments for the last 350 years. Hardly any chance of that, and for good reason. Who wants to admit their grandfather owned human beings and treated them worse than animals?"

"Sorta' the way a dog covers over his shit as quickly as possible, then moves on. He doesn't go back for a second look," I said. "Bobby used the phrase, 'covering the rotting corpse over with a white sheet.'"

"Exactly," Arthur agreed. "But in the case of man, the monster within is responsible for turning him into a beast. Lynchings, beatings, rapes—isn't that beastly behavior? Most aren't willing or able to look at themselves critically. It takes courage to grapple with the truth; not everybody's up to the task. So the mindset continues from generation to generation. In spite of Whites learning, directly or indirectly, to discriminate by color, not everyone falls in line. The trick is to determine who is biased." He pushed his glasses up, checked the time, and said with a grin, "Class dismissed."

He was right. To imagine any part of my family involved in slavery turned my blood cold.

Arthur reinforced Bobby's viewpoint, although Bobby had included a personal statement of self-loathing. Was that from being Black or having a poor self-image? Arthur didn't make a personal connection between the two. Maybe he was above such frailties.

Both agreed that White people had to address the history of slavery before having an honest discussion. Were they expressing a general consensus among all Blacks or just their opinion? I doubted my White contemporaries would agree. More than once, I'd heard, "Why dig up the past? What's done is done. Let's move on. Furthermore, I never owned any slaves."

I didn't think taking a deeper look into our history was outrageous. It was my belief that if we didn't learn from the past, we were destined to repeat it.

Bobby and Arthur widened my eyes to the degree of racism in America and how its history was hidden under the carpet to fester. What leader, Black or White, could convince America that it would be in her best interest to face the past, and start an honest dialog on how to move forward? Organizations like SDS (Students for Democratic Society) and SNCC (Student Nonviolent Coordination Committee) were supportive, but until they reached more than just a fraction of the Black population and a few White liberals, how could they affect real change?

Arthur took pleasure in shocking me with lesser-known facts of our history; the ones left out in American History 101. With a self-satisfied grin, he enumerated the contradictions going back as far as the writers of the Constitution and the Bill of Rights. "They all owned slaves as they carried on about the inalienable rights of man—but not the Black man. Most of the presidents up to 1867 owned slaves. And what about the systematic slaughter of the Native Americans to make way for the 'land of the free?'" Arthur chided. "The John Wayne movies weren't big on clarifying that the West was already occupied by the Indian Nations simply minding their own business, living in harmony with the land."

I was relieved that Bobby and Arthur could discuss race with me, but was perplexed at how they could spell out the inaccuracies in our country to a White boy who knew only privilege.

On a typical Saturday evening, the usual characters gathered on Soden Street. The familiar banter gradually evolved into a more substantial conversation on the best ways to advance the freedom movement. The discussion quickly focused on the three most prevalent philosophies—non-violent protest, responding to violence with violence and, finally, shoot first, ask questions later! The greatest support nationwide, but not necessarily on Soden Street, was for Martin Luther King's passive resistance, appealing to the moral fiber of White America to do the right thing. The country, I thought, should be hailing these people as living examples of what Jesus taught—love thy enemy. But no, too many saw the Black struggle for equality as a threat to White supremacy and privilege. While King's message of non-violence brought slow change, more aggressive approaches gained momentum.

The Black Panthers, still in their infancy, said "hell no" to turning the other cheek and reminded America that they too had a constitutional right to bear arms and would return fire if fired upon. But with only 23 million African Americans in a nation of nearly 200 million, I doubted they were looking for outright confrontation. The Panthers adopted Malcolm X's philosophy of self-determination and defense, which seemed reasonable. I was laboring to do the same, to determine my own future.

The third most aggressive approach to equality was headed by Stokely Carmichael and H. Rap Brown, who weren't waiting around for Whitey to see the light. Stokeley's expression: "Ready for revolution," put the fear of God into me and other White liberals. Brown went further, saying, "Violence is as American as apple pie" and "If you don't come around, we're gonna burn it down," leaving little doubt about how fed up he and others were.

As if intermission had been announced, the discussion paused. People got up and moved around. Someone changed the record, the fridge was raided, and Lucky rolled a fat joint. When everyone settled back down, a quiet man named Karl stood and waited for calm. Then, with great poise, he broke the silence.

"We're all after freedom, no doubt," he began. "But is it only for economic freedom, to be as materialistic as White society? A nice house and car would be hip, but the White man has *all* that and is still crazy. If we can figure out where they fell on their face, we can avoid the same mistakes. Too many brothers think the brass ring is a Caddy and a tailored suit. Spending money we don't have only keeps us in a different kind of slavery, with credit cards and banks as the bossman. With all the rhetoric about revolution, let's pause to understand what we want in life. If we have the chance for self-determination on a communal scale, we need to have a plan. Start with finding a deep sense of self, free from all the illusions the American Way has fed us; then maybe we can help ourselves as well as others. We should be figuring out how to fulfill our inner needs along with social justice. As descendants of the noble Ethiopian culture, the *True Human Beings*, why should we settle for mere material trinkets? We must move beyond the knee-jerk reactions of believing that getting more money or getting even will set us free. It makes me sick when I see a brother selling scag to another brother, keeping us in the cycle of spiritual poverty."

He took his seat and waited for a response. With such a departure from the usual smash-and-burn, everyone was speechless. Even Lucky was rendered silent. As the room emptied out, Karl apologized for breaking up the evening.

Unable to sleep, the phrase "a deep sense of self" repeated in my head. What avenues had I explored besides the music to know myself better? LSD dramatically changed my view of the physical world, but that was just an introduction to the mysteries of the beyond.

Coltrane's quest for higher consciousness was well known, and his music lifted me the way nothing else can. The challenge lay in staying at that level or, even better, surpassing it.

Bobby and I talked about the concentration required to venture further. Just when you think you're advancing, a distraction comes along to derail the process. His lament over Coltrane and Toni illustrated how slippery the slope can be. How can you stay focused if you're depressed?

With all these thoughts swirling in my head, I returned to the living room. Curtis Amy's new release, *Mustang*, sat beside the turntable asking to be played.

Bobby wandered out and sat next to me for our favorite track, "Shaker Heights." Leroy Cooper's baritone sax opened with haunting low notes, hitting me in the solar plexus. Often I can tell if the tune will grab me within the first few notes. Amy's soprano and Jimmy Owens' flugelhorn joined in to play the theme while the baritone continued laying down a bass tone that all else was built on. The soprano gave a great solo; then the baritone took over. Its deep, textured sound was hypnotic, opening my ears to this great instrument. The flugelhorn soloed next, its velvety sound a perfect addition to the baritone. This music wasn't celestial, it was just solid, toe-tapping jazz. With our eyes closed, lost in imagination, Bobby and I responded to the music as if we were in a club.

Inspired by the evening's discussion, we picked up the subject of struggling toward personal freedom. As we talked, I hoped Bobby might let something slip out about his inner turmoil.

Unfortunately, that wasn't the case.

He pointed out that the drive for personal freedom and freedom in music were the same. "The musicians we admire are moving beyond the boundaries of playing rhythmically or even harmonically. They want to fully express their inner feelings, which isn't possible in the framework of a tune. To some, this may sound non-musical, the way Shepp played at the concert."

Unsure of what he meant, I asked for another example.

"A jazz critic confronted Eric Dolphy with, 'Your music sounds like bird calls.'

Dolphy answered, 'I find bird song to be one of the most beautiful sounds on the planet, so thank you kindly for your compliment'"

"Dolphy straightened his ass out. Who else?" I asked.

"Most obvious would be Milford Graves playing the drums with tree branches."

"Are you serious?"

"Shit yeah! And another drummer, Andrew Cyrille, uses a violin bow on the edge of the cymbal."

"Who does he play with?"

"You're slippin' Wig—Cecil Taylor!"

"Oh, right."

"Keith Jarrett plucks the strings inside the piano," Bobby continued.

"Yeah, he did something similar on Cannonball's *74 Miles Away*," I remembered.

"Saxophone players routinely play chords. Ya know, Coltrane stacked chords during his "sheets of sound" period.

"Hold on. What LPs are we talking about?" I asked.

"*Soultrane, Milestones,* and *Giant Step*s for sure."

"Oh, right."

"All these cats are expanding the possibilities of expression. Words like energy, spiritual, metaphysical, and freedom have popped up to describe what they're doing."

Bobby concluded with: "This drive for freedom now shows up all over the place—fashion, painting, poetry, the anti-war movement—but I'm mostly aware of it in jazz. Some critics say all the chaos and noise on the street is now on the bandstand and called Free Jazz. But for those with ears to hear, there's a real quest for a spiritual awakening in that music. These guys are thinking outside the box, which is just what *we* need to do."

I agreed, but what interested me more was that his depression lifted long enough for conversation. I wondered if it would last.

Both Arthur and I had been selling small amounts of grass to people we knew for their personal use to supplement our meager cash flow. But we never found a reliable source to buy from in Boston. So when a friend of Dos' said he had a connection in New York and we could buy a pound from him, we pooled our money together and made our first foray to the Big

Apple. Back home, the goods were quickly distributed and we made a decent profit. Future excursions weren't just about business. More than once, we piled into the GTO late at night, music blasting, and headed down the Interstate to explore the New York nightlife.

On one buying trip our connection said there would be a few hours delay before the goods arrived. He handed us a generous sample of the product and suggested visiting the Electric Circus on St. Mark's Place or the Palladium on 52nd Street. By the time we arrived on St. Marks, I was pretty high. Inside we quickly tired of the electric pop scene and left for the Palladium. On the ride uptown we smoked another joint. The club, known as a swinging Latin night spot, was in full tilt when we showed up. The music and the dancers were out-of-sight. But I was too high. As Arthur hit the dance floor, I stood back, feeling light-headed. My legs began to buckle in the hot, stuffy air. I knew I would be on the floor any minute. Without an empty chair in sight, I turned to a woman seated behind me.

"I need to sit down...now," I pleaded in a feeble voice. "Please, let me sit!"

She'd barely stood up before I collapsed into the chair. Instinctively, I put my head between my legs to let the blood flow back into my brain. Arthur was working hard on the dance floor, watching the women's skirts lift as they spun. He thought he saw me but was distracted by all the stockings and garter belts. Who could see past that sight? Again, the skirts lifted. This time he saw me slumped over in a chair.

"What happened to Wigman?"

When I could sit up and take a few deep breaths, I lifted myself out of the chair and thanked the lady. She showed concern and warned me to take care and be aware on the streets. What an embarrassment! My debut in a New York Latin club, and I nearly passed out! I walked around outside until I felt steady enough to go back in. The possibility of dancing with this sharply-dressed crowd of flawless dancers was out of the question. At least I could appreciate the great music and ogle the women from the sidelines. On our return to take care of business, Arthur giggled, "Too high, my friend, too high."

CHAPTER 14

A PERSONAL SECRETARY

Arthur was a man of numerous talents. His ability to court multiple women at once certainly was one of them. However, the task of bedding all the eager young White girls at BU had become unmanageable. He needed someone to screen the incoming phone calls. Since I was in the apartment most evenings, Arthur thought I could act as his personal secretary. He gave me detailed instructions on what to say to whom. "His mother is sick"... "His car broke down,"... "A friend needed a ride,"...etc.

After a few weeks of overseeing Arthur's small harem, I'd had enough. Not that I was expecting a phone call, but it irritated me that all the calls were for him. Knowing his power of persuasion, confronting him would be tough. Finally, with uncharacteristic authority in my voice, I looked straight at him, "I'm fed up taking your calls, keeping track of what to say. I'm done! You figure the shit out yourself."

His reply, "You're right," caught me completely off guard.

"I am?"

"Without your help, they would have peeped my card a long time ago. The wrath could have been fatal, ya know? I'm in your debt and will make it right."

I was speechless. Where was Arthur going with this? Maybe fix me up with one of his spare women?

"What if I give you an ounce of grass a week to take my calls?" Arthur asked, showing great promise in his future profession as a psychologist. End of discussion.

Bobby and Dos laughed and asked how to get in on this deal.

With my nervous disposition, I decided to deal only enough grass to buy a new stereo amplifier. That happened quickly. I chose a "Scott Kit," meaning I had to assemble it. No big deal; I'd built one in high school. But back then, I didn't have these distractions—work, Carol, school, and constant socializing in the evening. One weekend, I told the merrymakers that the amp was nearly done and I'd hook it up soon.

"Great, we'll hang out 'til then."

Sometime after midnight, I announced, "It's finished. I'm turning it on."

The room fell silent. Enjoying the spotlight, I flicked the switch. A slight crackle accompanied by a puff of blue smoke came out of the amplifier, proving without a doubt that smoking pot and reading diagrams don't mix.

Steve, who was also studying electronics with me at NIT, found this particularly funny. "What would Mr. Wilkes have to say?" he asked, referring to one of our professors. The amp was in such a mess the factory had to sort it out. Quite a humiliation for a soon-to-be electronic technician!

Once the amp returned in working condition, ownership of the system gave me *some* priority over what went on the turntable. Whenever numerous people were in the room, all hassling to hear their choice, I might have the last word. Yet too often, I was buffaloed out of the way by trickery and fast-talking.

At about the same time, I decided to cut back my smoking to weekends only. With upcoming finals, I needed to focus. With too much loud music and pot, paranoia had set in.

I pleaded, "Put a towel at the bottom of the door to the hallway, turn on the AC."

"It interferes with the music."

"Well then, at least open a window."

"It's too hot/too cold. Sit down and relax."

"How about you smoke in one of the bedrooms?"

"But then we can't hear the music."

No one else showed concern.

Our cheaply constructed building lacked adequate insulation between apartments. One Friday night, around 2 am, the music was loud, and the air filled with reefer when our next-door neighbor, whose bed backed up to the wall where our speakers sat, came knocking on the door. Standing in his pajamas, he was greeted by smoke billowing into his face. He begged us to turn the music down.

"Oh yes, of course. So sorry." An hour passed before the volume was right back up. The others were oblivious to how critical this situation could become, increasing my paranoia. If I had been the neighbor, I would have called the cops. He never did.

CHAPTER 15

1968: A TURNING POINT

As the new year began, the country seemed eerily quiet, although little had changed except the weather. Doubtful that the calm would last longer than the snow, I still held on to my optimistic view that the war would deescalate, that Martin Luther King would find more traction, and that I would continue to thrive on Soden Street.

After completing our courses at NIT, Steve and I landed good jobs. My gig at Massachusetts Institute of Technology Labs was in walking distance. The work wasn't remarkable, but the pay was decent, enabling me to salt away a few bucks each week. Content with the circle I already had, I made little effort to make new friends at the Labs.

Sadly, Bobby's disposition didn't improve. To make matters worse, he began having difficulty paying his share of the rent. Our spontaneity from the Anderson Street days was now a distant memory. Only occasionally, when the atmosphere was conducive, with just the two of us listening to music, would I see glimpses of his old self.

In the last days of January, the Tet Offensive in Vietnam began. When the smoke cleared, the North Vietnamese hadn't gained a military advantage, but politically it was a different story. For the first time many Americans began to question their military and political leaders who continued to assure them the war would soon be won. Journalist Walter Cronkite summed up, "We are mired in a stalemate, and the only rational way out will be to negotiate, not as victors, but as honorable people who lived up to their pledge to defend democracy and did the best they could."

Alto saxophonist John Handy's 1966 album *Live at the Monterey Jazz Festival* became an enormous hit on Soden Street around this time. Not only was the music fantastic, but the LP consisted of just two long tracks, "Spanish Lady" and "If Only We Knew," increasing the chance for both the musicians and the listener to get into something. Naturally, when Handy came to the Workshop, we all went down, Lucky in tow.

Steve and Chops were already there, holding a front-row table. The audience energized Handy, and he and the band responded with fantastic music. Between sets, Lucky approached him and, in his usual assertive manner, asked—no, *told* Handy—that he would be coming over to Soden Street after the last set.

Lucky strutted back to our table. With index finger waving in the air, he announced, "Yes, well, what you don't know is, Handy will be joining us after the last set at our—*your*—crib."

We told him to sit down and stop with the bullshit.

"Okay. You'll see. Didn't I get Chico Hamilton to come over?"

Shortly after the music finished, Handy and the band came to our table asking, "What's happening?"

As soon as we all arrived on Soden Street, Michael White, the violinist, and drummer Terry Clark disappeared into Arthur's bedroom to snort coke. The others settled for smoking a joint with us in the living room.

Lucky, in prime form, ran his mouth about the beautiful evening and, of course, how astral their music was! Lucky and Bobby vied for Handy's attention, looking for the inside story.

When the joint was passed to Handy, he silenced the room by saying, "I've never really smoked before!" Nobody believed him. "The right occasion never came up," he said with his familiar smile.

"Well, Mister Handy, allow me the pleasure of rolling you a nice fresh joint," Lucky said, two-stepping across the room.

Good fortune had smiled on me once again. A hipper scene I couldn't have imagined. Handy and the others were at ease, sprawling out and asking for snacks. As Arthur and Dos told car stories to Bruce Cale, the bass player, Handy went through our records. "You guys have a solid collection here, more together than mine." Putting on Cannonball Adderley's *Somethin' Else,* he went on, "Cannonball was one of my first influences. And I see that Trane Lives in this apartment. "Digesting all Coltrane left for us will take a *long* time."

Everyone was engrossed in conversation, so I decided to act as the host serving them. The poetic justice in serving a room full of African-Americans didn't escape me. Bobby hovered next to Handy, listening as he told the behind-the-scenes story of his appearance at the Monterey Jazz Festival in '65. After a local jazz critic had sent John Hammond of Columbia records a tape of Handy live from The Both/And Club in San Francisco, Hammond immediately came out to California and insisted

Handy play at the festival. The recording (*Live at the Monterey Jazz Festival*) put Handy in the national spotlight. I sat close by, hanging on every word as if I was auditing a class in advanced music theory.

By dawn, Handy wanted to go back to his hotel. As host, I drove the band in Arthur's car to the Hotel Vendome on Commonwealth Avenue. In our elevator, I noticed Handy donning the very smile that appeared on the cover of his latest LP, *New View*, cementing the night into my memory.

When they got out of the car, Handy casually said, "Oh, I must have left my horn at your apartment!"

How does a horn player forget his horn? Either he was too high or was just incredibly mellow. But it gave me more time to talk with him.

When I finally returned home, Lucky and Steve were still there. Everyone agreed this night was one for the books, and we congratulated ourselves for pulling it off.

Lucky pranced around like a peacock. "Well, well, Handy knew from the start that I was one of the beautiful…"

"Look, man, you did good! Don't fuck it up now with your beautiful people rap. Give it a rest," Bobby said.

CHAPTER 16

LUCKY IN HARLEM

Lucky's "flavor of the week" girlfriend, Lynda, mentioned driving to NYC. He was going with her to visit his father in Harlem.

"Harlem, I've never been there," I said. "What's it like?"

"Come with us and see."

"Man, I'm definitely up for that. Your father won't mind?"

Early Saturday afternoon, Lynda dropped us in Midtown. On the "A" train to Harlem, I asked Lucky if he knew Ellington's well-known song, "Take the A Train." Avoiding a clear answer, he said we could visit where Ellington lived, but it was a long walk.

Before getting off the train he said, "Get yourself together for Black Mecca." I felt every muscle tense up, not knowing what he meant.

Harlem gained notoriety in the 1930s when people in the arts flocked uptown to experience the Harlem Renaissance. There were more swing clubs than you could count. By the mid-sixties, much of its glory had faded, but Harlem remained *the* center of Black culture.

Once we emerged from the subway station on 125th Street, I thought I saw the famous Apollo Theater.

Lucky quickly fell into his "guide" persona and confirmed, "Yes, yes, and just past it, that tall building is the famous Hotel Theresa. We'll see it all. First, let's drop our bags at my father's."

He talked non-stop as we walked, but I didn't hear a thing. I'd been under the illusion of gaining some sophistication during the past year, but I felt like a hayseed again here in Harlem. Harlem might not require a passport for entry, but it was another country. The streets were filled with every shade of black, brown, and beige, with rarely a White face in sight. Countless times I'd been the only White in the room, but to be the only one visible in this thriving metropolis was monumental. Under Lucky's wing, fear didn't interfere with the experience. With sunglasses on to conceal my wide eyes, I stole a page from Lucky's book and looked around without moving my head.

At first I compared 125th Street to Washington Street in Roxbury; there was no comparison.

Lucky's father's apartment, off 7th Avenue, was in a typical New York six-floor walk-up. Harold greeted Lucky in a casual but hip sort of way. They bore no resemblance; Harold was tall and slender with a light complexion and wavy slicked-down hair. His pencil mustache and pressed shirt and trousers gave him distinction. He acknowledged me with a glance and a nod.

His lady friend Ruby was more hospitable. Younger than Harold, darker, dressed in a housecoat and slippers, she covered her afro with a colorful scarf.

Eager to see the city, we dropped our bags and headed for the door. Harold gave Lucky a key and a five dollar bill—"At Ella's, put five on 339."

Did anyone notice my jaw drop? I certainly knew about numbers, but I'd always thought it was an activity conducted in the shadows of the night. Here it was as commonplace as buying a bottle of milk!

Back on 125th, I noticed Lucky peering over his shoulder and hesitating as he rounded a corner. Was he being protective, or nervous that his past might be waiting for him on the next block?

On our way to the Apollo, I checked for reaction to my presence on the street. So far, nothing. Lucky listed off the many performances he'd seen at the Apollo, mostly R&B and soul. Just down the street, stood the Hotel Theresa. Known as Harlem's Waldorf Astoria, it was frequented by Black entertainers or visiting politicians who couldn't stay downtown. After he left the NOI, Malcolm X had his headquarters for the Afro-American Unity there. Lucky knew how to impress me by pointing out Castellan Hair Salon on 125th, where Miles Davis and Cicely Tyson were patrons. Frenchy's reputation extended far beyond the borders of Harlem, attracting jet-setters from downtown. I slowed my pace for a look, hoping to catch a glimpse of the man with his horn. The last stop on our lightning tour was the famous Lenox Lounge where Coltrane, Miles, Billie Holiday, and many others had performed.

"It's time for a meal," Lucky announced. "We'll be dining at a deluxe restaurant in the neighborhood."

"Do you think that's wise?" I asked, not wanting to push my luck.

"Have you felt uncomfortable or threatened so far?"

"No."

"This is going to be a trip! The diners will wonder what the hell you are doing up here; let's see how they check you out."

Oh great! I thought. *So far, I've managed to be inconspicuous. Now he's going to parade me through as if I were a circus act.* But no one stopped eating to gawk as the maitre d' showed us to our table in the corner, perfect for us to watch the diners, but not so easy for them to watch us.

Lucky whispered, "They wanna look, but they're way too hip to be obvious."

Since no one took exception to my presence, my nerves settled enough to focus on the significance of dining on 125th Street. Who could I impress with my story of getting over in Harlem? The boys back home would just shrug, "Oh, yeah, that's cool." Certainly not Gary or Scotty, maybe Leigh if he was around.

Walking back to the apartment, Lucky was unusually quiet, giving me a moment to reflect. If the tables were turned, I wondered, if I took Lucky to some WASPy restaurant in Wellesley or Brookline, would he be treated as well?

Back at the apartment, Lucky and his father disappeared into the bedroom to sort out some business. I sat with Ruby in the kitchen around a green and white Formica table with chrome trim. While she made tea, I took a closer look at the room. The appliances were old, the walls dingy, and a buzzing circular fluorescent ceiling light cast its blue-white glare. The window facing the air shaft was covered with a film of grease. A picture of Jesus depicting him as an Arab hung prominently. I'd never seen Jesus depicted as Middle-Eastern; I appreciated it. The tiled floor, now broken, was patched with concrete. Once Ruby sat down, she didn't bother with small talk.

"Where did you grow up? Is Lucky the only Black person you know?"

I didn't feel interrogated; she was just being direct. The curiosity was two-way, but being in her house I treaded into the conversation carefully.

Hearing I was born in a small New Hampshire village without a store, she responded, "That's a long way from 125th Street, and I bet there weren't any Black folks up there either. So how do you know Lucky?"

"In Boston, through a friend."

"You know other Blacks?"

"My three roommates are Black."

"Oh, that's good. Is Boston more integrated than New York?"

"I can't say about New York, but Boston isn't as progressive as I would prefer."

"What's your job?"

"I just started working as an electronic technician, and…

"Good money?"

"Decent."

"Well, I was born and raised here. But unlike you, I've never lived anywhere but in Harlem. I wouldn't mind going somewhere different. But where and do what? These streets are all I know. I got folks in South Carolina, but… This city can be so hostile; there was a terrible riot here only a few years ago. And that Bumpy Johnson is running drugs and numbers like nobody's business!"

"Who?"

"Oh, Bumpy's a big-time gangster in Harlem. He's nice enough if you stay out of his way. I have it in my mind that our friend Lucky might have crossed one of his soldiers, the way he up and left in such a hurry. Harold never told me. Maybe he doesn't know, either. Best not to mention Bumpy to Lucky."

Ruby sat back in her chair, lit a cigarette, and looked right at me, "You're all right…" ("for a White boy" hung in the air without being said).

Before I could ask her how many White people *she* knew, she went on surprising me with personal stories of her broken marriage, not having kids, and lack of job options. Ruby made it clear that Harold wasn't the ideal companion, but he wasn't abusive the way her husband had been.

"I don't mind that much about the kids, though it would be nice to have someone to look in on me when I'm old. With all the chaos on the street these days, I'd be a fool to depend on that."

I muttered, "All you can depend on is death and taxes."

"Now ain't that God's honest truth," she said, pouring more tea.

Why was this older woman opening up to me? Here I was, an alien in a strange land, and Ruby was comfortable unburdening herself. For whatever reason, I was flattered, even honored. When Lucky and his father emerged, she abruptly stopped talking. I thanked Ruby with a smile, hoping she understood how grateful I was to have a moment with her. She returned the smile as she cleared away the dishes.

I joined the men watching the nightly news in the living room. The flickering television was the only light, but it was enough to get a sense of the room: heavy curtains hiding the window bars, a framed photo of Malcolm X, a beat-up side chair, and the black-and-white TV with rabbit ears balanced on a flimsy card table. The floor was oak or fir—so worn and dirty, who could tell? The three of us sat on the sofa in silence, pretending to care about what was happening on the screen. Lucky's demeanor with Harold—only speaking when spoken to—was not that of the Lucky I knew.

We pulled out the sleep sofa when Harold and Ruby went to bed. But there was no way I could sleep with impressions of Harlem running through my mind. I made the motion of smoking a joint to Lucky; he nodded and pointed up. We eased ourselves out the door and up the stairs to the roof. It was magic with all the street lights and noise rising into the night sky.

"This is a perfect end to a day I could never have imagined," I said, taking a long draw on the joint.

"Well, well, I knew you were hip enough to meet Harold and Ruby. And—and tomorrow, you'll meet my mother."

Lucky carried on as I drifted out over the illuminated cityscape. A line from Allen Ginsberg's *Howl* came to mind: *Angel-headed hipsters dragging themselves through the Negro streets looking for the ancient heavenly connection to the starry dynamo in the machinery of night.*

I didn't know what it meant, but the quote fit the moment. As Ruby said, "This is a *long* way from a village in New Hampshire!"

The lights from 125th Street shone brightly, but the towers of lower Manhattan radiated a mystical glow, floating between heaven and earth. A city so vast, all dreams, all failures, and every type of human behavior could be found on these streets. How exciting! How terrifying!

Back in the apartment, we had the munchies. Too lazy to go out, we settled for a bowl of cornflakes. Trying to sleep, one of Ruby's comments rang the loudest. "Look at this place, do you think this is what I imagined when I was your age? I can't even remember what I thought, but it wasn't this."

Everyone was up early on Sunday. Ruby made coffee and toast but said little with Harold at the table. Before we left, he gave Lucky a few last words of advice. I got the same nod Harold gave me on arrival. He must have wondered what his son was doing with this honky. With her back to Harold, Ruby gave me a sweet smile. Going down the stairs, I asked Lucky if everything was cool.

"Shit, yeah. Why you ask?"

Sunday morning—the only people on the street were all-nighters staggering home and sharply dressed churchgoers.

The streets weren't the least intense; I strolled with Lucky, full of confidence. For a moment, I congratulated myself on how quickly I'd adjusted. But the first down-and-outer eyeballing me brought reality back in a hurry.

We met Lynda in Midtown and she drove us up to New Rochelle. Lucky directed us through an upper-middle-class neighborhood where his mother lived. Predominantly Black, it bore no resemblance to Roxbury. We stopped in front of a small single-family home, all neat and trim, with a white picket fence. Hard to imagine this was where Lucky's mother lived. The door flew open as we approached to ring the bell. There stood Beaver's mother June Cleaver (*Leave it to Beaver*)—except Black! I thought I was having an LSD flashback. On closer look, I could see it was Lucky's mom all right. She was short and stocky like her son, the same complexion but conservatively dressed, wearing an apron. Elated to see Lucky, Mabel gave him a big hug and a kiss. I tried to visualize her with "Mr. Slick," Harold.

"I'm so happy to meet Lionel's friends." She was probably the only person who called him Lionel. "Won't you come in?"

Inside was even tidier than outside. This aspiring street hustler had a mother right out of '50s Hollywood living in a mirror image of White suburbia. I was in a state of shock. Once again, Lucky's persona changed—this time to an affectionate son in his mother's company. Would the real Lionel Francis please stand up? In her well-appointed living room, she served fresh lemonade with homemade cookies. This was another one of those moments when I expected Rod Serling to appear from the other room saying, "You have just entered the Twilight Zone."

Mabel asked what I did for work. "Oh, that's nice!" she told me. And then she praised Lynda for attending BU. Lucky turned on the charm, insisting he was poised for a breakthrough job coming any day now. I suspected she must have known this wasn't true. The time spent with Mabel was sweet. Watching Lucky with his mother, who adored him, was worth the trip alone. She packed sandwiches and cookies for the drive back to Boston.

This weekend had far exceeded expectations. Walking the streets of Harlem, and hearing Ruby's story, followed by the contrast of Mabel's life in New Rochelle, were experiences I would never forget. To say my awareness of Black life in America had greatly expanded wouldn't begin to cover it. I wanted to express this to Lucky, but true to his character he blew me off by saying, "Well, well, you're one of the beautiful people."

On the trip back, March 31, we heard on the radio that President Johnson would *not* run for another term. We were jubilant at the prospect that this would hasten the war's end in Vietnam, but our optimism was short-lived.

CHAPTER 17

APRIL 4, 1968: RIOTS
AND DISILLUSIONMENT

Martin Luther King was assassinated Thursday evening, April 4, in Memphis. I heard sirens wailing down Western Avenue all night, but gave them little thought. Early in the morning our phone started ringing next to the couch where Dos slept.

Annoyed, he answered abruptly, "What!" followed by, "Oh shit," resounding through the apartment.

Arthur opened his door to hear. "They shot Martin Luther King dead last night."

Bobby jumped up, dressed, and left with the others without a word.

Terrified, I cowered in bed, refusing to think about the ramifications—open warfare between the races. Work seemed irrelevant, and who wanted to venture out with retribution in the air? When I finally looked out the window, all appeared deceivingly calm. No armed gangs roamed the streets looking for blood. I flicked on the radio for a reality check. Sure enough, riots were erupting in nearly every urban center. In Washington, DC, mobs closed in on the White House, and 28 blocks were demolished in Chicago. The news wasn't helping my mood. I turned it off.

I knew the constantly ringing phone wasn't for me, so I took it off the receiver. I looked around the apartment, wondering if I had a future here. Where would I go? And what about Bobby? The others could manage, but this might be too much for him. I played Coltrane's *A Love Supreme*, but he failed to lift my spirits. When the doorbell rang, I ignored it. No one was coming to see me. The buzzer wouldn't stop. *Who the fuck....? Oh, maybe the boys left so quickly that they forgot their keys?*

My heart sank when I recognized the voice—Bobby's friend Romy. The man with the mounted rifle. "Where's Bobby? Arthur? Where's Dos?"

"Out."

Silence, then, "I wanna come in. Buzz me in, man."

"Nobody's here."

"BUZZ ME IN!"

Too feeble to resist, it was my destiny to hear his wrath. Red-eyed and sweaty, Romy marched through the apartment. What did he expect to find? He gave me a penetrating stare as I slowly sat at the far end of the sofa, hoping he'd leave before his anger seriously messed up the only White person in sight.

Then the floodgates opened, releasing a torrent of verbal venom. There was no escape from Romy's inflammatory monologue detailing the barbaric behavior inflicted on him and his ancestors ever since they stepped off the boat in the New World. "And what about the do-nothing politicians and trigger-happy police?" He made his point repeatedly to ensure I got it. What could I say? *Oh, no, you have it all wrong. There's no prejudice here; everyone respected King. This was just an isolated nut with a gun. You'll see, justice will prevail.*

Eventually, grief overtook his anger. Romy looked blankly across the room, covered his face, and wept. I came out of my self-protecting mindset to witness this militant hardass in tears. I not only heard his rage, but saw first-hand the heartbreak that my friends were going through. King's assassination dragged people into this turmoil from across the political spectrum. Romy's position was far more radical than King's, but that didn't diminish his despair. His tirade wasn't necessarily directed at me, but we both knew that, as a White man, I was complicit.

Exhausted, he stared out the window, then left.

The room vibrated with silence.

Back in my bedroom, I curled up in a fetal position.

The boys would be back soon, hopefully with their hostility tempered. How would they feel about living with a White boy now?

As the sun sank, so did my spirits. Today's events illustrated that goodwill amongst friends wasn't enough to bridge the chasm of racism. How could I begin to fathom what they were experiencing? Ever since I'd connected with Bobby and the others, I had no illusion of seeing the world as they did, but I wanted to widen my perspective and learn how others navigated through obstacles different from mine. I lulled myself into believing that an open mind and heart *could* eliminate distrust and prejudice. James Earl Ray's bullet had burst the bubble I'd created of living in harmony. I supposed it would have happened sooner or later; I'd been hoping for later. Now there was no turning back to such a naive philosophy; this was the real world, filled with misery, greed, and hate. What was it going to take for people to wake up to the fact we all bleed red, we all inhabit this small planet, and that all people deserve a chance to live their lives without being terrorized?

Arthur and Dos returned first. Looking angry and spent, they spared me the details of their day. It was as awkward as I'd feared.

Bobby came in late with an expression between anger and guilt. I asked no questions, just relieved everyone came back in one piece.

At the end of that tragic day, there was a bright moment. Boston remained relatively calm compared to so many cities in flames, largely thanks to James Brown. Previously scheduled to perform at the Boston Garden that evening, Mayor Kevin White was convinced James should go on as planned. The Mayor persuaded WGBH to broadcast the show live, keeping more people off the street. No one consulted James. He was furious hearing about it, knowing ticket sales would plummet. He demanded $60,000 in compensation. The city managed to stall, and the concert went on as scheduled, without an agreement and to a much smaller audience. When Mayor White walked on stage to introduce James Brown, the Mayor needed reminding who James was—a sign of how out of touch White was with the Black community.

The concert was a resounding triumph in spite of a crowd of fans swarming the stage, nearly setting off a confrontation with the police. Only through James' persuasion did order prevail. The band members later said they feared the whole place would go up in smoke.

The sad footnote: the city never compensated James for the weak ticket sales, netting him only $10,000 with no expenses. James commented, "Well, *we* did the right thing." Moving on to war-torn Washington DC, he continued his peacekeeping concerts around the country in tribute to Dr. King.

In the morning, Arthur read a quote from an underground paper: *White America killed Dr. King last night. She made it a whole lot easier for a whole lot of Black people today. There's no longer a need for intellectual discussion; Black people know they must get guns. White America will live to regret that she killed Dr. King last night. It would have been better if she had killed Rap Brown or Stokely Carmichael, but she lost when she killed Dr. King.*

Hearing this prediction, the hair on my arms stood on end. I left the room and called Carol.

"Come right over," she said. Until now, the fact she was the only White person I hung out with had little relevance; now it seemed a godsend. She understood my awkward situation on Soden Street.

Carol's apartment faced north with no chance of direct sunlight, but she'd made the best of the gloomy living room by hanging colorful curtains on the windows and a braided rug from Goodwill on the floor. She greeted me with open arms. The aroma of freshly brewed coffee wafting out of the kitchen added to my composure.

Pouring a cup of coffee, she said, "Please tell me exactly how you feel, don't hold back." Holding my hand, she encouraged me to be honest with her.

"Alienated! Estranged from my best friends," I replied. "Once again I'm reminded that, ultimately, we're alone, even when surrounded by friends. I first faced universal loneliness back in the mental hospital, then promptly forgot about it when I met everyone here. Now that reality is back in my face. Am I exaggerating? What do you think?"

A long pause followed. Then she said, "I want to share my life with someone, but…"

"It's the *but* I'm talking about."

"We *are* alone," Carol agreed. "Just individual beings drifting through life. Never will two become one. I don't want to think how impossible it is to know what another person is thinking. Keeping track of my own thoughts is difficult enough. I want to go into this deeper with you, but dealing with King's assassination is occupying my mind right now, and yours too, for sure.

Have the boys been hostile?"

"No, but I can't imagine how they feel about me living with them."

"Best not to project, just take it a day at a time and see how they act around you. You'll know what's the right thing to do. The country—your friends—may never fully recover, but time will soften the edges, and we *will* move forward," she said.

The rest of the morning was spent stating the obvious—the divisions and hatred in our country and how King's death had thrown gas on the fire. By noon, Carol and I needed fresh air and a change of conversation, but first we went up on the roof to see if nearby Cambridge Street was in flames. All looked reasonably calm, and we ventured out for lunch. In the restaurant, a television showed one horrifying scene of destruction after another. Everyone had an opinion:

"King was getting too big for his britches."

"Just when King was making headway, some nut with a gun."

"There's too many guns."

"I'm getting a gun today; no nigger will get me."

We ate our spaghetti and went back to the peace of her apartment. After a night in bed with Carol, I felt more relaxed. The morning news clarified that random violence in Boston had ended, so we went out for a walk pretending all was normal again. Passing a large record store, Carol suggested going in. I pulled out a few LPs but hesitated to blow money during a time of such uncertainty. "Just buy what you fancy; the albums will be a good icebreaker back on Soden Street," she urged. I happily took her advice and grabbed Coltrane's *OM* and *Cosmic Music*, hardly easy listening—but what was easy these days? Then I saw the cover of Andrew Hill's *Grass Roots*, two young boys, one Black, the other White, having a great time playing together. I had to have it regardless of the music.

Back on the street, I hugged Carol, thanking her for encouraging me. "Now, what would *you* like?" I asked.

"I'll show you when we get back to the apartment," she said grinning, then slowly ran her tongue across her lips, giving them a wet sheen.

I grabbed the nearest lamp post to steady myself.

She laughed, "But there's no hurry. Let's keep walking. That'll give more time for imagination."

The afternoon light faded. It was time to face the boys back on Soden Street. Carol's parting advice, "Let them bring up King's assassination if they want. Otherwise, avoid the subject."

I hesitated outside the apartment door, listening for clues about what reception I might expect.

As soon as I entered, Arthur and Dos caught sight of the LPs under my arm and said, "New music? What have you found?"

Bobby rushed out to see, "Oh, Trane! And Andrew Hill *with* Lee Morgan!" Surprisingly upbeat, he grabbed all three albums saying, "Just what is needed today, new tunes." Eager to hear Lee Morgan, who had been out of action for a year, we played Andrew Hill's *Grass Roots* first. Everyone responded to the album's glad-to-be-alive vibe. Carol was right—music was a perfect way to re-enter this delicate situation.

When Andrew Hill finished, I leaned over to ask Bobby if he wanted to hear Coltrane's *Om*.

"You need to ask? Let's see if Trane can blow these blues away."

Om started with a chant, then slid into a chaotic free passage.

Dos and Arthur disappeared out the door with a "later."

Coltrane, Pharoah, and McCoy Tyner gave less than remarkable solos. The whole piece meandered. We agreed the chanting didn't work, but there were moments when the music came together reminiscent of *Ascension*. The liner notes by Nat Hentoff confirmed this music wasn't easy. *Start by letting the music come*

in without preset definitions of what jazz has to be, he advised...
*once heard and absorbed, these sounds lead to further extensions
of listening and feeling capacities...In Coltrane's music, there's
an increasing preoccupation with the meaning of life, for the
absolute necessity for compassion and mutual understanding...*
What a perfect time to hear this!

"Don't we have to let go of the anger before we can be compassionate?" I asked.

"Easier said than done, there's so much anger out there. But my issue is depression. Well, maybe I'm angry with myself too."

Why hadn't I considered that? Last summer, Bobby had mentioned low self-esteem, but I thought it was because of racism. This sounded different, relating to something he'd done, rather than a reaction to outside forces. Bobby's anger could be compounding his sorrow over Trane and Toni.

Bobby continued, "As for the meaning of life, you know I've been struggling just to get through the day. That's about all the meaning I can handle right now. What are your thoughts?"

"Could you say more about your anger?"

"Gerard, I will, just not tonight. It's a deep subject, and with King's murder weighing on me, I'm not up to it. But I'm curious to hear your thoughts on the meaning of life?"

"There *is* meaning," I said with certainty, "but the challenge is to be conscious of your path and follow it. We may be reincarnated souls working through a particular problem unresolved in our past life. I have a strong belief in reincarnation. What do *you* think?"

"Like Johnny Griffin said, *If it's real, I must've messed up big time to be born into a world with so little love.* I wonder what I did to deserve this heartache? So I guess I do believe in it."

Bobby's expression signaled the end of our conversation.

I let it drop, grateful for the listening session and his willingness to engage at any level, allowing me to see the Bobby I knew and loved still existed beneath the weight of his sadness. We agreed to wait until tomorrow to play *Cosmic Music*.

The following evening, Bobby was down in the dumps again, showing no interest in hearing the other new Coltrane album, but I insisted. We unwrapped the gatefold LP to study its contents. Inside, there were two black and white collages. One was with Coltrane and Martin Luther King; the other was of four figures forming a cross: A crucified Jesus, two Buddhas on the left and right, and the sphinx below with the Om symbol in the middle. Then we noticed that the credits listed his wife, Alice Coltrane, on piano and Rashied Ali on drums.

"McCoy and Elvin were replaced? "Why?" I wailed.

Bobby had read that McCoy Tyner felt drowned out after Pharoah Sanders had joined the band, and Elvin Jones had continually missed gigs. Rashied was always waiting in the wings for an opportunity to sub for Elvin, and his perseverance paid off. Coltrane asked him to join the band. I immediately copped an attitude about the new lineup that Coltrane had put together toward the end of his life, but Bobby said, "Be cool, let's hear how they sound."

The first track, "Manifestations," began with a blistering solo from Coltrane; Pharoah followed on piccolo. This was the most intense piece from Coltrane to date, but shorter than we would have prefered. The following track, "Reverend King," was also strong, featuring Coltrane on bass clarinet and a more convincing chant than on *Om*.

Yet I was still bothered about the absence of Elvin and McCoy. Coltrane had often added musicians to the band, but this was a dramatic shift, especially with Alice on piano. Trane never gave us time to catch up, he had been continually moving further into uncharted territory. Now that new music was being released posthumously with a different band, he continued to challenge my ability to keep up with him, even after death. With the country coming apart at the seams, I was looking for stability, not more hurdles to overcome.

Bobby read my mind, saying, "Do you think Alice and Rashied sound okay with Trane, or was it a big mistake?"

"I don't know, this recording is great, but I miss Elvin and McCoy no matter how wonderful the new group sounds."

"I can dig it, but it's Trane. He knew what he was doing. It's up to us to follow the Trane, wherever he wanted to take us, right? You know what Shepp said about Coltrane?"

"No, but you're going to tell me, right?"

Bobby picked up a copy of *Down Beat* magazine and read, "He was our mentor, freeing Black music from the entertainment syndrome. Black musicians were always told they had a certain amount of time to do their thing. Coltrane decided to play as long as it took; sometimes a matinee could last three hours without a break. It's a challenge, Coltrane is still a challenge."

"Right on, Archie Shepp," I exclaimed. "Trane's music is Free, expanding time and space."

I suggested listening to the LP again. This time with less bias.

Afterwards Bobby asked, "What do you think about it now?"

How Bobby's mood had improved over the last hour, from disinterest to fully engaged with Coltrane's new music, was remarkable. Other than jazz, I hadn't seen anything else that could lift him out of his despair. I wanted to keep the conversation going in hopes it might morph into a personal dialogue about his inner state.

I started, "When I first heard Miles' *Jazz Track* when I was only ten years old, I could recognize the language. After that, it took time to expand my "vocabulary," but these new recordings have elevated my experience. This album triggered a deeper spiritual reaction in me than *Om* or many other recordings I've heard, *A Love Supreme* being the one exception, with its poem to the Supreme."

"Brother, I completely agree, but tell me more about how it affected you spiritually."

"When I say spiritual, you must understand I have no practical experience other than my LSD trip, so I use the word loosely. The music is more than mental, more than emotional, so *is* it spiritual? Let me tell you a short story that might express better what I'm trying to say. When I was a child, a daily train from Boston passed through Tilton, New Hampshire. Three miles away, up on a hillside in Sanbornton, I played in the cow pasture behind our house, often alone; my imagination was all I needed. When the train wound its way through the valley, the whistle from the old locomotive, caught in the wind, floated over the trees, up to me on the hillside. That sound created such a reaction in my gut it was almost painful. I had no connection with trains, but something welled up, forlorn but more complex. Why, I had no idea. The sound of train whistles still haunt me. I felt a similar overpowering response listening to *Cosmic Music*—a sound that resonated in my soul. I don't mean like Smokey Robinson singing about the 'Tracks of My Tears.' A response is there too, but I'm thinking of something less obvious."

"Great image of you sitting on a hill listening to a distant train whistle. Keep going," Bobby said.

"Coltrane's music is universal."

"Absolutely! Universal Trane! Remember when we started our listening sessions, you had little to say other than whether or not you dug the LP? Now you express yourself with ease and your insights on Coltrane are right on. He *does* play music of the soul, he's caught the Sound of the Universal God, and we are blessed to hear it," Bobby extolled.

I wanted to hear more about the Sound of the Universe, but Bobby lifted himself off the couch and disappeared into the bedroom.

There was too much rattling around in my head for sleep as I wondered about the Sound of God. If there was such a thing, I felt we should all have access to it, connecting us in a celestial song. This was much more appealing than wrestling with human isolation.

The boys had been better tempered than I'd presumed. No one mentioned the assassination, and thankfully, there wasn't a wall between us.

A day later, I remembered Bobby's comment about being angry with himself. I ran through a few possible scenarios for his anger; maybe he'd had sex with Toni's best friend, hit her in a violent argument, stole the family's jewelry, hit a pedestrian while drunk. None of these rang true, but how would I know?

He'd promised to talk about his anger, and I anxiously awaited for that to happen. If Bobby could open up about his "deep issue," it might turn the tide.

The week following King's assassination, communication in our apartment remained stunted. Everyone was trying to remember what life was like before the slaying of King. Bobby's mood bounced from sullen to agreeable, then back to silence. He must have forgotten about discussing his anger with me.

Arthur curbed his confrontational rhetoric, showing empathy for how I was feeling, but being a political creature, it left him with not much to talk about.

Dos communicated little, even at the best of times.

Lucky dropped by but never mentioned King or the riots, which seemed odd. Still, I was happy to see him; listening to his new scheme for fame and fortune gave me a sense of normalcy.

Steve and Chops also never mentioned King's death or how they dealt with it. I didn't think they were shutting me out though. It just wasn't the time to have that conversation. The time might never come, and that would be all right as long as we remained tight. Until now, I depended on them for guidance through *my* dramas; this time, I'd have to go it alone.

Soden Street continued to be a hangout. The only difference was me—I kept further in the shadows, only speaking when spoken to. The conversations were predictably more heated. With the loss of Dr. King, the radical parts of the movement, SNCC for example, became more significant. There was a lot of bitterness in these discussions causing me to withdraw into my room. Huddled on my mat one night, bits of a conversation floated in from the living room.

"Maybe through the force of our struggle, African-Americans will turn out to be the saviors of America—politically, culturally, and morally." I nearly jumped up with applause, so happy to hear something positive.

Then came, "What White people don't know about African-Americans is what they don't know about themselves," followed by, "If they shot King, who tried to work with the White establishment, who's next?"

The country didn't have to wait long for the answer.

As tempers calmed, I fantasized that life would revert to "normal"—for me and the country. But how would that be possible? I wondered.

The fracturing of America continued on June 6th when Robert Kennedy was assassinated in Los Angeles. An outspoken critic of the war, he had energized young voters, including many of Dr. King's followers. The country reeled from the loss of two leading peacemakers in rapid succession, and now another Kennedy had been wiped out.

If Nixon won the nomination, who could successfully run against him? Both the left and right agreed that the country was having a nervous breakdown. In my view, most of the current negativity could be attributed to the recent loss of optimism. The hippies saw their vision of utopia dissipate, Blacks were fed up with the lack of civil rights reform, and much of the country was sick and tired of the war.

Kennedy's assassination created less of an upheaval on Soden Street than King's, defined by Arthur's comment: "As Malcolm X said, 'The chickens are coming home to roost,'" and Dos' one-liner: "Now they're beginning to shoot their own."

Bobby showed little reaction.

All I could see was more violence.

On Friday afternoon, I grabbed my toothbrush and went to Carol's; I knew she would be upset. She usually cared little for politics, but RFK had captured her imagination. "I believe he could've made a difference, picking up where JFK left off. He felt like one of us. Now *who* will stand up against the war and discrimination?" she asked, not expecting an answer.

I suggested a walk along the Esplanade. On the river, small sailboats skimmed silently across the water, calming our minds. We sat down to watch the colors from the sunset dancing on the water, turning Carol's hair auburn. Ours wasn't a big romance, but we enjoyed each other's company and appreciated having each other to lean on, especially during one crisis after another. We expressed our anxiety over how bleak the future looked.

She asked if I had any alternative plans.

"Plan? I have no plan besides putting one foot in front of the other. But I'm going to start saving every dime I can," was my instinctive reply.

"Save for what, a car?" she asked.

"No, just save. We should have a backup strategy in case of a meltdown."

By the end of the weekend, we had soothed each other's nerves and felt better about facing the upcoming week.

I was thrilled when Bobby said, "Let's go over to Franklin Park and hear Duke Ellington." The concert was part of Elma Lewis's *Playhouse in the Park* program she'd started in 1966. Lewis opened the School of Fine Art for underprivileged children in the old synagogue overlooking Franklin Park, which I remembered from our late-night tours of Roxbury.

Bobby and I joined the mostly Black crowd of five thousand giving the Duke an enthusiastic welcome. This was the first time we'd seen Ellington and were thrilled to be there. Bobby bumped into friends; they high-fived and laughed.

Instinctively, I hung back, hoping he would engage and not just put on a happy face.

A light-skinned brother, Fred, had a particularly aggressive stance; even without hearing what was said, his body language was provoking. On the bus back home, I asked Bobby about him. "Oh, Fred is a starving artist, pissed off about everything but mostly the color of his skin."

"What?"

"It's another Black thing; we can discuss it later."

Then he sunk into the dark place that had become so familiar, staring blankly out the bus window.

CHAPTER 18

A HANDFUL OF PHENOBARBITAL

Walking back one day from a long, tedious day at MIT, I noticed Arthur hustling Bobby into his car behind our apartment. The drama wasn't obvious, but it didn't look like they were going shopping either; it appeared to be an emergency.

"What happened? Where are you going?" I asked with apprehension.

"He just downed a handful of phenobarbital," Arthur said with irritation and concern.

I jumped in.

Bobby stared at the floor and groaned.

I desperately wanted to say something, but words failed me. Instead, I held his hand, feeling his slow heartbeat. *If he dies,* I thought *...no, I'm not going there. But what if he does? Could I ever forgive myself knowing I failed to help him when he desperately needed support?*

Bobby's groan motivated Arthur to step on the gas, and we flew down Storrow Drive. At Mass General ER, a nurse placed Bobby in a wheelchair and rushed him away.

Arthur gave information to the front desk, asking when we could pick him up.

"You'll need to talk to the admitting doctor tomorrow."

On the way back, Arthur filled me in. He'd found Bobby doubled up on the bathroom floor, holding a bottle of pills. Arthur admitted his first reaction was frustration. "What the fuck, more drama! But looking into Bobby's pathetic face, I couldn't help but feel his pain. Man, watching him wince, holding his stomach. How messed up do you have to be to swallow phenobarbital?"

"Did you see this coming?" I asked. "Bobby has been *off* for too long—but not like this! What do you think prompted it?"

Arthur flippantly suggested this was another desperate act to win Toni's sympathy. "The brother has a screw loose." He said no more.

The lack of Arthur's usual monologue indicated his concern.

I replayed everything Bobby had said and done recently for hints, but nothing stood out.

Dos came in shortly after we got back. He shook his head. "Poor Bobby is going through some heavy shit." Unable to say more, he walked out of the room. That evening we went to an Indian restaurant for a change of scene and agreed to hold off assuming anything until we heard from the doctor.

Images of Bobby choking down a handful of pills—*where did he get them?*—kept me restless all night. How could I have been so oblivious? He must have assumed I was too fragile to confide in. Now the comment about his anger took on a new dimension. Wasn't attempted suicide a violent and angry act?

I should have been direct. *Look, man, I know you're suffering. Tell me something so I can help. Stop pushing me away.*

Until now, I'd refused to think of Bobby as emotionally unbalanced, but this changed my mind. How desperate and self-obsessed he must be, caring little for those who loved him.

In the morning, Arthur called Mass General. The doctor confirmed they'd successfully pumped Bobby's stomach, and he was in recovery. Since this was an attempted suicide, he would be sent to the state hospital in Bridgewater for observation. We could visit him there during the week. Relieved at the good news, I wondered if the state hospital would help. But without health insurance, there was no other option.

This latest episode had me tied up in knots. I couldn't connect the person to his actions. Bobby, my closest friend, had attempted suicide and was now in a mental hospital. Not long ago, we'd spent the evening absorbed in Coltrane's new releases the way we used to on Anderson Street. During the week of Bobby's absence, nobody mentioned how to handle his return. Personally, I needed advice. Even Carol had little to offer.

In my room, looking at his empty bed, my emotions flipped from sympathy to irritation. Here I was adjusting to life after two assassinations that sent ripples of impending doom across the country, and now I had to deal with the disastrous effect that Bobby's suicide attempt had on the love I felt for him. But aggravation towards him was short-lived, as I realized he was slipping through my fingers like sand.

The three of us drove down to visit him in Bridgewater. On the way, Dos tried to make light conversation by mentioning that Albert DeSalvo, the Boston Strangler, had just been transferred from Bridgewater to Walpole. That news fell on deaf ears.

Then Arthur picked up the ball, referring to a recent documentary film shot in Bridgewater called *Titicut Follies*. A Boston judge had permanently banned it in Massachusetts for its blunt depiction of the 19th-century practices used. "Oh, great!" I said,

"This is where Bobby is supposed to find help?"

The hospital was a sprawling complex of gloomy, run-down Victorian buildings, enough to make a "normal" person feel depressed. In comparison, Concord Hospital in New Hampshire, where I'd spent a few weeks, was a country club. Any hope for Bobby leaving this place healthier looked slim.

Entering the main building, the place reeked of unwanted lives left to wither. But Bobby greeted us as if he was on holiday. Joking about the deplorable conditions, he kept the atmosphere cheerful.

Everyone played a part, unable to face the cold reality of why he was there and what had prompted him to take all those pills.

I felt utterly inadequate, only able to say, "Hope you're managing all right here," and "Can't wait to see you back in the apartment."

On the ride home, I mentioned how pathetic Bobby looked in his gray uniform. Both Arthur and Dos just nodded. On the silent ride to Cambridge, I searched for an easy answer to how my dear friend had nearly committed suicide. His actions were a desperate cry for help, but he needed to open up to us or a private professional, or even to someone at Bridgewater.

Our visit showed no signs of any such opening.

Bobby's homecoming was without fanfare. He crept in during the day when we were all out, then disappeared. Staying in the apartment even less than before, he avoided any chance for us to connect. Where he spent his nights remained a mystery. Like a boat with its mooring cut, I watched him drift away.

In Bobby's absence, I cornered Arthur in the kitchen. "He's no better. Bridgewater was a waste of time. He's shut me out even more than before. How can I help if I don't know what's going on? You still believe this is about Toni? You two go way back; aren't you concerned?"

Arthur looked up with a sigh, "Course, we're concerned! And I wasn't right saying that was a stunt for Toni's benefit. At that moment, I didn't want to think too deeply about it. But this sorry event has got me rethinking Bobby being gay and…"

"Whaaat?" I heard myself say. "Gay?"

"Hell yeah, you didn't know? We suspected back in high school. Bobby's never been openly gay around us, but some of his friends were light in the loafers," Arthur said with a smirk.

"No, I didn't know! And why are we talkin' about loafers?"

"You know, gays!"

Showing my irritation, I said, "What's the matter with you two? Didn't it cross your mind to share that insight with me? It might have helped me understand some of his bizarre behavior. Although I'm not convinced."

"We shoulda' run it by ya, sorry Wig," Dos said. "We're cool with it, never gave it much thought. But since Coltrane died, it must have shaken somethin' loose down deep."

"And when Toni gave him the boot, it must have pushed him over the edge," Arthur speculated. "This became clear to me when we saw him in Bridgewater."

Avoiding any apology, Arthur explained that being Black is a liability that can make people crazy from the get-go. "Being gay adds to the burden; it's enough to make anybody crack. Bobby doesn't need to be put under a spotlight either. Don't ask too many questions," he cautioned.

"Questions, shit, I haven't seen him long enough to say hello." Wanting to pick holes in their theory, I asked, "Then why did he shack up with Toni and get so bent-out-shape when it ended?"

Arthur peered out from the kitchen, his glasses halfway down his nose. "It's probably more complicated than we realize. He could be bisexual or trying to convince himself he's straight."

"This ain't the '50s. There are plenty of gay men who deal with it just fine. Why can't he?" I wanted to know.

"Yeah, maybe. But still, being gay ain't easy," Arthur continued. "You can't go home and say to your parents, 'Hey Mom, Dad, I'm shacking up with my boyfriend, Bill. You wanna come over for dinner?'"

"Well, you're right." I agreed. "Remember how upset my mother got when she heard I was living with Carol for a few months? What if I'd said I was gay and moved in with Rodney? Society is still a long way from accepting gays. The strong ones don't give a fuck, but I bet most are still in the closet."

"Wig has a point," Dos said. "We don't know…"

"No, we don't," I interrupted. "I'm not convinced he's…"

"I'm not trying to convince you of anything. You asked, and I'm telling it the way I see it. Okay?" Arthur said with an attitude.

"Something messed him up to pop all those pills!" Dos added.

There was no denying that. I retreated to my room to ruminate over what the boys had said. If Bobby was gay and his friends hadn't made a big deal about it, then why did I immediately reject the notion? Maybe because I didn't want to acknowledge how much goes over my head. Or maybe my anxiety about homosexuality stopped me from seeing what was right in front of me. Bobby probably noticed my angst and kept the subject off the table. All of the nights he was out probably weren't with Toni.

During the days and weeks that followed, Bobby remained distant, denying me any opportunity to communicate or offer support. His body language said, "We can talk, but at a safe distance, don't push!" Now I finally understood what Carol had said a while ago, " He needs to choose to change."

Since the pill episode and Robert Kennedy's assassination, both Soden Street and the nation were in a holding pattern, which was an improvement over the continued slide into chaos.

My Uncle Bob offered me (and my friends) his house in Sanbornton for the weekend while he was in Vermont for an antique show. When I suggested the idea, Arthur's girlfriend Karen was the first to show enthusiasm. "Escaping the city heat sounds good to me!"

Karen was a sweet lady from Maine—blond, delicate, and charming. Soft-spoken, she rarely got a word in with the men running their mouths non-stop. Fully aware of Arthur's small harem, Karen had faith that things would change for the better. I didn't have the heart to tell her otherwise.

Arthur went for the idea of a weekend in the country too, but Bobby showed little interest. I thought he'd jump at the chance to meet my parents but the idea of being cooped up in the car with us, being asked about the rent, or prying into his nightlife, must have put him off.

Dos agreed, "Yeah, man, let's go see where Gee-rah's from." But at the last minute, he couldn't go.

When Lucky caught wind of our plans, he wanted in. "Well, what you don't know is, just cause I'm a brother from Harlem doesn't mean I can't get over with country folk."

I had high hopes for this therapeutic weekend in New Hampshire. On a beautiful Saturday morning, we set off in the GTO. Once on the highway, we cruised along to John Handy's "Spanish Lady," with fresh air blowing in the windows. In Sanbornton, Lucky greeted my parents as if they had been friends for years. His flattery abounded. "How wonderful to meet you. I've known Gerard for a long time, he's a good friend and speaks of you often. What a beautiful old house… blah, blah."

Even my far-from-streetwise parents realized they were in the midst of a snow job in August. Dad, always a welcoming host, thanked Lucky. My mother did not engage and asked, "Who would like iced tea?"

Lucky eased inside the house with me in close pursuit. He admired the antiques, the wood beams, and the large fireplace, saying, "Yes, well, I can dig it, a vintage New England house." Was he honestly inspired or just taking mental notes to further his next country exploit?

Before joining them on the terrace, I peered through the kitchen window at my parents sipping iced tea with my friends. Déjà vu! This scene had played out years ago with Rodney. The difference this time was that I had more confidence in myself.

A grade school friend, still living in Sanbornton, invited us to meet in Old Hill Village. A flood-control dam downstream had forced the town to be abandoned in 1941. Now only cellar holes and an abandoned bridge remained. In this pastoral setting, Lucky shifted gears from city slick to "by the riverside jive." He had us all rolling in the grass with laughter. My school friend watched as if a traveling road show had come to town. "Who is he?"

On the ride back to the house, Lucky pointed out, "What you don't know is, I'm a man for all seasons, all situations, and all people...as long as they are 'the beautiful people.' Can you dig it?" He could, and on this day in my hometown he was at his most entertaining.

We spent the evening in David's studio above my uncle's antique shop, smoking grass, listening to jazz, and studying David's abstract paintings, all very bohemian.

The next morning, we drove to Belknap Ski Area to ride the chair lift to the observation tower. Looking north over the Lakes Region and up to the White Mountains, the view inspired

Lucky. With his finger waving, he elaborated on the beauty and the expanse of blue and green. He could have been perfectly sincere, but unfortunately anything Lucky said was impossible to take seriously. On our ride back to Boston, he pointed out how cosmic it was to meet my parents after I had met his.

The summer had been fraught with assassinations, riots, and attempted suicide. Few had escaped unscathed. Spending a weekend near a river in New Hampshire was a Balm of Gilead.

One evening after work, Arthur announced he wanted soul food: fried chicken, black-eyed peas, candied yams, and cornbread. "Let's go to Bob the Chef's."

"Yeah, but…"

"Don't worry," Arthur assured his dubious vegetarian friend. "I'm sure they'll have plenty for you to eat."

The cafe was located somewhere in the South End. Inside, I scanned the large deli case. As I suspected, the server looked blank when I asked for a vegetable plate.

The place was packed.

As usual, I was the only White face in the joint. I couldn't help but overhear the conversation behind me from our booth.

A group of African-American men were exchanging ordinary stories from their day. What I heard was not only the solidarity between those sitting at the table, but within the whole community, among all Blacks across the country. Expressions like, "That's right, bro," or "Dig it, my people," sent waves of exclusion through me. How odd to have this reaction now and not during one of the many contentious discussions on Soden Street.

After dinner, we rode around the neighborhood. Failing to think before speaking, I blurted out, "The conversation I overheard in there, brother this, our people that, reinforced the idea of how I'm an outsider. I am, of course, but…"

Arthur interrupted, "Huh, guess you know how Black people feel."

I couldn't hide my embarrassment for saying such an absurd thing to a Black man. "Sorry, Arthur, for being so thoughtless."

"No, it's okay. You identify with us but aren't one of us. Interesting how that happened." He launched into his theory of how Whites are brainwashed from an early age. The status quo instills the idea that the White race is superior to all others, which has proven highly effective in the US and any place where people of color live.

"You missed that class, didn't ya?" Arthur joked. "Living up there in the country with no diversity, most everyone else swallowed White supremacy without a second thought. Why didn't you fall for it? Were your parents hip to the propaganda?"

"They were good parents. I'm not aware of them spelling out equality directly, but if prejudice came up, my mother quickly put it down. My father didn't go for it either, but he was less vocal," I said.

"Didn't you hear nigger this…nigger that…in high school?" Arthur probed. "Didn't you go along to get along? I bet they thought you were strange."

"Yeah, I heard it, but with only one Black in our class, it wasn't much of an issue. Of course I was viewed as weird in high school, listening to jazz, becoming a vegetarian, and being lousy in sports and academics. But the positive influence from the music saved me. When I first heard Miles Davis he became my first hero, then came along Coltrane, who blew me away. Through the music, an affinity grew toward something outside my own community. Thanks to you all, I've had the chance to expand beyond the boundaries of my race and society. When I left high school, all I wanted was to be in the city, to find friends and jazz. Man, that worked out much better than I'd hoped."

"But the question still remains," Arthur said. "How did you avoid indoctrination? If you figure it out, bottle it for mass distribution. And putting up with us Black folk during these bizarre times, you must have felt threatened once in a while."

"Romy was pretty intense," I acknowledged.

"Romy can be, especially after King was shot."

"And your light-skinned friend, Fred, seemed to have a short fuse too."

"You know why, don't you?" Arthur asked.

"Yeah, Bobby explained to me the dynamics of skin color within the community."

"Light-skinned people catch shit from from the militants for not being Black enough, reminding them how many have White ancestors and, of course, the Whites don't want 'em either," Arthur concluded.

I wanted to make up for my inane comment by saying how included I did feel with them. "Through you, Bobby, and Steve, my perspective of the world and myself has opened up to embrace what I couldn't have imagined just a few years ago. I'm not the same person who first walked into Bobby's apartment."

CHAPTER 19

MORE THAN A BAD DREAM

A month had passed since Bobby's stay in Bridgewater. With no improvement in his behavior, I took solace in the fact that he hadn't declined further. But my patience had worn thin waiting for him to be frank with me. Bobby opened my heart and now he was doing a good job of closing it.

Bobby asked me to walk up to the Harvard Coop to check out the new LP releases. It was a perfect afternoon, reminiscent of so many walks we'd taken through the streets of Boston when our thoughts and feelings flowed freely. But not on this day. By the time we reached the Coop, Bobby hadn't revealed anything. I only bought Miles Davis' latest release, *Miles in the Sky*, keeping the purse strings tight.

On the way back, I encouraged Bobby to beat the bushes for a job. "Having a schedule would be good."

He quickly replied, "Yes, I have an interview next week."

Wait a minute, I thought. *This sounds like Lucky.*

We put on the new Miles LP which failed to initiate a conversation. I was disappointed but not surprised. Since the pill episode and confusion about his sexuality, my connection with Bobby once again included fear. Initially, I feared race would tear us apart, but now the fear was for his well-being.

Late one night, I dreamt a hand was in my underwear, and then it wrapped around my dick. As I slowly rose out of deep slumber, the dream persisted. When my eyes opened, I realized, "This isn't a dream. It's happening!"

I bolted upright to see Bobby lying beside me, his hand stroking my johnson. "What the fuck are you doing?"

Like a turtle retreating into its shell, Bobby rapidly withdrew. His face buried in a pillow, I could scarcely hear him say, "Sorry... I'm so sorry."

My whole body shook with anger. How could he be so devious to come on to me in my sleep? Face-to-face would have been more honest. Sneaking around in the dark was a complete breakdown of our friendship.

I was about to chew his ass out, but then the ramifications hit me like a brick. I lay back down and kept quiet.

He's messed up!

Did he think I was interested in sex with him?

Or was this another self-destructive act?

When my head stopped pounding, I realized my response could have been better than "What the fuck." More rational replies came to mind, but they were useless now. Tomorrow I'd tell Bobby we *must* talk, no more waiting.

In the morning, Bobby's bed was empty. He must have gone out early to avoid embarrassment. My confrontation would have to wait.

I made my way to the bathroom and turned on the light. What I saw could have been an outtake from *Psycho*. Bobby lay naked in the bathtub, his wrists slashed, blood sprayed everywhere. Above him on the wall, the words "I'm sorry Gerard" were written in blood. My mind flew away for several moments in disbelief. Then reality came crashing in.

"Arthur! Dos! Come quick, Bobby's done it again!" I yelled.

Holding my breath, I inched forward. Thank God he was alive, although barely conscious.

Arthur took one look and immediately shifted into action. He tore his T-shirt up to make tourniquets.

Dos grabbed Bobby's clothes. Without sharing a single word, the three of us moved in sync. Scantily dressed, we ushered him to the elevator.

In the back seat with Bobby, I held his limp hand as we sped to Mass General Hospital ER—the same as a few weeks ago. Over and over, I said in a low voice, "You have nothing to be sorry for. We will get through this."

Dos and Arthur remained silent.

Fortunately, the nurse was not the same one as before. She laid Bobby out on a gurney and disappeared.

Arthur gave Bobby's information while I peered around the ER, wondering if we were stuck in some bizarre loop in a parallel dimension.

As I calmed down, I started to understand Bobby's violent act wasn't only self-destructive; he'd included me in his nightmare. Bobby knew my morning schedule, I would be the one to find him. So this was either a cry for help or punishment for my rejection.

Arthur wanted to know what "I'm sorry, Gerard" in blood was about.

I downplayed Bobby's groping, in no mood to dump on the poor guy.

"We told you…"

"Arthur, this can't simply be about sex. He's acting out a confused call for help. If he just wanted sex with me, this had to be the most ridiculous way to go about it. No, I'm sure of that."

They half-heartedly agreed.

The reason why cleaning the bathroom fell on my shoulders escaped me. Looking at the scene where Bobby's limp body had lain, head resting back on the bathtub's rim, eyes closed, I felt nauseous. In a disembodied state, I quickly removed the bloody message. His blood circling the drain mirrored our relationship. How could I have prevented this? He needed help, and I'd failed him. His blood lodged under my fingernails, and I didn't attempt to remove it for a week.

By day's end, the hospital called. Bobby had survived. He'd received a blood transfusion and was now sedated and would be going to Bridgewater for at least thirty days as soon as he could travel. A collective sigh drifted through the apartment. Dos voiced what we were all thinking, "Maybe he is ready to accept help now."

But was Bridgewater the right place to find it?

"At least he's safe down there," Arthur added.

My anxiety didn't evaporate because he'd been placed in a state hospital for a month.

The following day, the three of us agreed that Bobby should *not* return to Soden Street. This latest suicide attempt clearly illustrated how serious his emotional state was and how ill-equipped we were to help him. If there was a next time, we might not be so lucky, and who wanted to deal with *another* death?

Both Arthur and Dos, knowingly or otherwise, showed unusual concern for me. My attachment was no secret.

Lucky displayed genuine worry.

Shaking his head in disbelief, Steve said, "The brother deserves better than Bridgewater."

None of us had the heart to go into the depressing details. What would be the point?

The month without Bobby slipped away slowly. Everyone who came over felt his absence. "Where's Bobby at? I'll catch him on the rebound."

In spite of desperately missing him, this allowed me to step back and look at the reality of our tattered relationship. I questioned how to proceed, if at all. My heart said hang on to the closest friend you've ever had. But my mind cautioned, *keep a distance until it's clear what direction he'll go, self-destruction or self-help. But if Bobby isn't living with us again, how can I tell?*

My room and the apartment took on a hollow vibration. Bobby hadn't died, but something had.

Life continued. Music still filled the air. Dos and I went to work and Arthur attended his classes at Boston University, but we silently grieved. Being true to our male nature, our sorrow wasn't expressed directly but through faraway gazes or downcast eyes. My internal strength had eroded over the past few months. Suddenly, Carol's question from a while ago, "Do you have alternative plans?" hit home. I was adrift, without direction.

Needing a diversion, Karen, Arthur, and I went to the première of *The Thomas Crown Affair* with Steve McQueen and Faye Dunaway at the Astor Theater on Tremont Street. Shot in and around Boston, the city looked deceivingly calm and beautiful in the film.

Arthur loudly expressed his approval for Thomas Crown's ability to string Vicky Anderson along while she thought otherwise. The cat-and-mouse game between them was familiar territory for Arthur, who was still maneuvering his small harem.

At the end of the movie, when Thomas Crown narrowly escapes, leaving Vicki behind. She looks up at the plane flying over Boston with tears running down her face.

Arthur jumped up shouting, "That's right! She thought she was so damn hip. Fly away, my man!"

We'd expected Arthur to be notified about Bobby's release, so it came as a surprise when Bobby showed up unannounced while I was at work. It was clear that he had no intention of running into me and trying to explain. Gathering up his belongings, he'd left without so much as, "See you around sometime," knowing we'd run out of patience with him.

When I heard he'd come and gone, I was furious. How could I hold on to any empathy for his burden when he showed no concern for me. But I still loved him.

CHAPTER 20

THE DEMOCRATIC CONVENTION
IN CHICAGO

On August 20, 1968, Soviet forces invaded Czechoslovakia, crushing all resistance in order to "restore and maintain law and order."

Arthur laughed, "The Russians use the same tired old language as the cops do here."

The waves of oppression blew across the sea and settled down in Chicago where the Democratic Convention to nominate the presidential candidate was scheduled to begin on August 26. Fearing the worst, Mayor Daley warned of dire consequences if protesters marched to the convention at the International Amphitheater.

In the days leading up to the convention, about 10,000 hippies, Yippies, and all other anti-war demonstrators began gathering in Lincoln Park. Yippie organizers Abbie Hoffman and Jerry Rubin played the press like a fiddle, announcing their plans to send hippie chicks to seduce the delegates and put LSD into the water supply. Mayor Daley took the statement as gospel, setting the stage for one of the major TV events of the year.

The fiasco started on August 25. The Mayor had set a curfew in Lincoln Park for 11 pm, and at exactly 11:01 pm, the police and National Guard stormed the protesters with tear gas and billy clubs. In the same way as in Vietnam, the TV cameras caught all the action for the evening news—picture after picture of young men, their heads bleeding, kicked by combat boots, and dragged off.

While we watched the events unfold on TV, Arthur pointed out that we'd seen this behavior before when the police "maintained law and order" in the ghetto, but few had paid attention. Now that the sons and daughters of White middle-class America were getting their heads bashed in, the country stood up to take notice. The violence was as excessive as the times.

Reporting from the convention floor, Walter Cronkite said, "Chicago is virtually a police state." Later the police defended their violence by saying the protesters shouldn't have broken curfew.

I couldn't keep watching this obscenity of the police declaring war on its own citizens. Any hope for a turnaround in the country or for me personally had vanished into a cloud of tear gas. I fled to Carol's for the weekend.

Of the two well-known responses to stress—fight or flight—the latter was more to my liking. I toyed with quitting my job and driving around the country in a van. Subconsciously I knew that traveling in the midst of the conflict wasn't much of a solution. But my narrow horizons limited me from considering anything more adventurous. I mentioned my plan to my mother and nearly fell out of my chair when she said, "But you've already gone across the country twice. Why don't you go to Europe?" I never imagined *my mother* would encourage such a far-flung idea. Just when you think you have a notion of who your parents are, they throw a curveball. Neither one of them mentioned that leaving my "career" after only nine months would look bad.

Europe has a definite ring—it has to be better than the US, I thought. Certainly not a paradise with Paris and Prague under siege, but the Vietnam War wasn't their headache, and as far as I knew, Europe was more racially tolerant. Many American jazz musicians lived there to escape "the American way of life."

A family friend asked, "Are you going to Casablanca for the winter?"

"That's a fantastic idea. You know that's one of my favorite movies—I'll do it."

What I needed was a new perspective and I hoped Europe and North Africa would give me that.

David, who had traveled to Europe twice, gave me a few addresses in England, Italy, and Greece. The decision was final, *at the end of September, I'm outta here.*

As I started packing my belongings, I confided in Arthur. "Even with the commotion on the streets and Bobby freaking us out, leaving is far from simple. To say goodbye to my friends and Soden Street is no different than splitting up a close-knit family. It's the end of a special period in my life. The planets will never line up to let this happen again. In some ways, maybe that's a good thing, right?"

"Wig, you don't need to explain," Arthur said, striking a serious tone. "Nothing lasts forever. The world is changing around us just as we're changing. It's been a horrendous year, but we survived. Europe won't be clear sailing either, ya know."

"For sure. I'm worried about only speaking English, but that isn't stopping me."

"If you don't go, you'll always regret it. And winter in North Africa? Shooot! See what those Arabs are into. We both know if Nixon wins the election, all hell will break loose. But I'll be here, reporting from the front lines, navigating through the deceit and lies pumped out daily."

Knowing how stressed I was, Carol had asked me to move in with her for the last month before my departure, rent-free. She and Katie now lived on Hemenway Street in Boston, and I jumped at the opportunity to be with her. The change of pace was like going from a Corvette to a VW bug. No more visitors knocking on the door day and night, little jazz (I'd stored my stereo and record collection in New Hampshire), and very little pot smoking. I was in withdrawal from Soden Street. Carol and Katie's apartment reverberated with the sounds of Janis Joplin and Blood Sweat and Tears. Where was Coltrane when I needed him? The shower rod was covered with pantyhose and underwear whenever I went to the bathroom. After living with three men, the adjustment to sharing an apartment with two women was a hurdle, but I was grateful.

Arthur made regular pit stops to see how I was holding up.

On my way to the Boston Public Library on Boylston Street to do some research about Morocco, I saw Paula, the folk singer, sitting in a cafe by herself. Ever since her legendary dance with Rodney on Anderson Street, I'd wanted to know her better, but her occasional visits to Soden Street had never given me the opportunity. I asked if I could join her. Our conversation quickly turned to Bobby, whom she'd seen since he'd left Cambridge.

"Paula, please tell me how he is. I worry about him."

"Well, since you asked, Bobby isn't doing well. He's out of work, moves around with nowhere to call home, and is all messed up about being gay."

With no quick response, I waited for her to continue.

"Bobby hates being attracted to men and tries to convince himself otherwise," she continued.

"What about Toni? Did he love her, or was it all an act?" I asked.

"No, he *does* love Toni, but I would say his body is in conflict with his heart."

"It was obvious he was suffering, even before the suicide attempts, but he wouldn't let anyone in to help," I replied. "We used to be tight..."

Paula interrupted, "He didn't go into detail, but he told me he regretted how your relationship ended."

"I certainly do too! I've never had a friend like Bobby and probably never will again. We clicked right from the start. How often does that happen? I'm still working through what happened, and I miss him terribly. I desperately want to reconnect with him, but it'll have to wait until I return from Europe."

"Oh really, Europe? What brought this on?" she asked.

"I hardly need to tell you what a disaster this year has been. Starting with the war, King's assassination, and all the rioting that followed. Then Robert Kennedy's murder, the fiasco in Chicago, SNCC, and the Yippies. In the middle of all this, Bobby nearly dies in our bathtub! It's time for a change of scenery."

"I can dig it. I wouldn't mind splitting myself if I get my singing gig together. Hope Europe works out for you 'cause we ain't seen the end of the chaos yet," Paula said with a glum expression.

"I'm glad Bobby's hanging with you. He needs..."

She cut me off, "Yeah, trouble is he's not around all that much, and it's hard to break through to him. But he's a brother, and I'll do what I can."

"I want to see him before I leave. Can you reach him?" I asked.

"No, I only see him when he drops by. I've got no idea where he's crashing."

"Oh, well, tell him we met, and I wish him the best. I really do."

As I walked away, the whole ghastly event in the bathroom replayed for the millionth time. I wanted to find closure, but couldn't stop thinking about him.

At the beginning of September, two weeks before I was to fly out, my old friend Leigh reappeared from England. When he heard my plans, his initial excitement faded.

"I just landed, and you're leaving?" But he quickly started supporting my decision. "I understand why you want to leave here. Strangely enough, those are the reasons I wanted to come, to see for myself."

When I fretted over traveling alone, Leigh reminded me how well my solo trip across the country had been. "Not to worry, my friend, you'll be fine once you meet some other travelers."

"But I only speak English. How will I manage?" I worried.

"It would be helpful to speak French or Spanish, but that didn't slow me down. Plenty of young people have learned English, DON'T WORRY!" Leigh reassured.

Then I asked him to explain why he'd come back.

"Besides Paris or Prague, this is where it's all happening, and I want to see if America can survive. There would have been a better chance if Robert Kennedy had lived. The US is in *deep* trouble, but the energy here draws me like a moth to a flame," Leigh said.

"Flame, all right! This whole country is about to go up in flames."

"What can I say? I had to come—destiny."

Once Steve heard what I planned, he said, "You're not leaving me behind. Shooot, you're not the only one who wants outta here!"

I knew I couldn't put much stock in his words though. Last summer, his promise to meet me in Frisco never panned out. So I prepared to go.

I acquired a passport, an international driver's license, and a certificate of employment from MIT Labs.

Leigh said the more documentation, the better.

Despite Leigh's assurance, I agonized at night about my lack of language skills. I should've paid attention in my French classes! But our teacher, right out of college, was hopeless, and I couldn't see the point at the time. My narrow horizon had been only Boston and jazz.

Chops, now living on Anderson Street, gave me a going-away party. The usual characters showed up. Even Carol made a rare appearance. The boys surreptitiously ogled her long legs, accentuated by her short mini-skirt.

Chops announced, "Wigman will be the DJ tonight. What's the theme?"

"Contemplation," as I put on McCoy Tyner's classic of the same name. This was the first party thrown for me since grade school birthdays and I enjoyed myself.

A few weeks later Arthur and Dos invited me over for pizza. They were full of encouragement, "Yeah, man, get the hell out before Nixon wins the election and the shit hits the fan." In their unsentimental way, both expressed how they would miss me. Without my stereo and paintings, the apartment resembled yesterday's news. I ate and left.

After his stint in Vietnam, Gary had landed back in his home-town of Lebanon, New Hampshire. Leigh and I drove up to see him. On the way, I related how Gary had questioned my choice of friends.

"Forget it," Leigh said. "The war scrambled his head. I don't think his question was as loaded as you think. And who knows when you'll see him again? Let's not get into anything contro-versial. We'll hang out for the afternoon, then leave."

Leigh was right. The three of us goofed around, smoked a joint, and listened to pop music. When Gary put on the *Sergeant Pepper* LP, he told us of an urban legend: If you wrote down all the numbers mentioned throughout the album, they would make a phone number. If you dared to call the number, it would be a real freak out! With little else to do, we made numerous attempts to come up with a ten-digit number. Eventually one surfaced with a New Jersey area code. Since we didn't want to pay for some bogus long-distance call, we decided to make it person-to-person (an operator-assisted call to a specific indi-vidual). But to whom? This was my going-away gig; I'd do the honors by calling *myself*. We could hear who answered the phone in New Jersey and since it wouldn't be *me*, we'd have a good laugh and not have to pay for the call.

The operator came on. "Yes?"

"I want to make a person-to-person call to Gerard Wiggins."

"One minute, please. The number is ringing, sir."

A man's voice answered, and the operator said, "Person-to-person call to Gerard Wiggins."

"Yes, this is Gerard Wiggins speaking."

Both Gary and Leigh could see the shock on my face. They said, "WHAT?" in unison.

I swallowed and started to explain to this older-sounding voice with my name, on the other end, how I had his phone number. The more I said, the more ridiculous it sounded, even to me. Frantically I tried to engage him, saying I was about to leave the country for an indefinite period of time but wanted to stay in touch. I could write from Europe. He was polite but declined, saying good luck and good-bye.

I hung up the receiver, saying, "Can you believe that? I just talked to Gerard Wiggins!"

We contemplated the odds in silence. Then I said, "Maybe I just talked to myself in the future or in a parallel dimension?"

"Was I right that this would be a freakout, just like our first LSD trip and the Moby Dick float outside our window on Fairfield Street?" Gary exclaimed.

We flared up a joint to either calm ourselves or find more insight; it let us down on both counts. The '60s were ending, full of confusion, division, and violence. But thank God the magic of that time in history still lingered in the air.

On the way back, Leigh and I stopped to see my parents. They unceremoniously wished me a safe journey. Why were they more comfortable with my departure than I was?

During my last days in Boston, my anxiety peaked. Carol working all day left me with nothing to do except fret over not having a solid plan.

In the evening I asked her to come with me to the Jazz Workshop where Freddie Hubbard was playing. Living together for the past month, we had grown close, but she understandably withdrew as my departure approached. She declined.

Music shared with friends always sounded better to me, but I had to go alone this time. "Alone" was the new me, so I had better get used to the idea. As soon as I walked in, I saw Bobby sitting against the wall by himself. I went right over and sat down. This was the first time I'd seen him since—well, I didn't want to remember that scene right now.

He looked surprisingly good, better than Paula had described.

As Freddie tore the place up playing "Birdlike," we smiled, acknowledging the unseen hand that had brought us together again. When Freddie finished his tune, we both stumbled over what to say.

Bobby broke the tension by launching into a tale of traveling across the country and having just returned a few weeks ago.

That didn't fit with what Paula told me, but maybe she didn't know.

"It was just what I needed, get out there and let the sun shine on my face. I met some hip people out on the coast too. Maybe I should have stayed. There ain't shit happenin' here. And what's shakin' with you?" Bobby asked.

"I quit my job at MIT and moved out of Soden Street."

Before I could continue, he said, "That's good. Now what?"

"After the Democratic Convention showed what a farce the election and this government is, I decided to split for Europe." The words hung in the air as Bobby tried not to show his disappointment.

"Oh, when?"

I paused, feeling I was deliberately hurting him by saying, "In a few days."

"Huh, how long are you going for?" he said with a forced smile.

Deadpan, I replied, "I have no idea. I'll stay until something else comes up. I've saved quite a bit and I'll work whenever possible. I'm nervous as hell to be going alone, but it's time."

Now avoiding eye contact, he eventually said, "I'm happy for you, but will miss you. What do you hope to find?"

"I'm looking for what has gone missing here, a more positive outlook. It's dark in America right now, and I'm still young and impressionable. All this negativity is messing me up."

"I can relate to that for damn sure."

"I'm interested to see how people in Europe and North Africa figure out their lives and navigate through obstacles different from mine."

"North Africa? I would dig going there!" Bobby lamented. "I hear the music is incredible. You'll have lots of stories if you ever come back."

The club was emptying out; it was time to go. On the street, we hugged, both wondering when our paths would cross again. I held Bobby so tight I felt his heart beating. The same heart that nearly stopped not so long ago. I thanked him for all he'd done for me emotionally, intellectually, and spiritually. "I started down the long road to becoming an adult under your guidance."

He tried to blow it off, but I insisted, "No man, you've been the closest friend I've had, and I still love you. Always will."

Once again, Bobby's face expressed more than words as he spoke in a low monotone, "I love you too." He turned and walked away.

It was heartbreaking to say goodbye to my dear friend and jazz guru. But I consoled myself that there couldn't have been a better way, sitting in a club listening to jazz. As he disappeared down Boylston Street, I knew we could and would resurrect our unique relationship when I returned.

September 27, 1968, the day of my departure finally arrived. Arthur, Gloria, Steve, Leigh, and I packed into the GTO for the ride to the airport. In the parking lot, we had some laughs, passing a joint around while Curtis Amy's "Shaker Heights" played in the background. With my friends close at hand, my nerves stayed in check.

As we said farewell, Steve assured me he had a plan and would be coming. I wanted to believe him, but didn't. Leigh insisted on flying to NYC, where I would pick up my connecting flight to Iceland. At Kennedy Airport he gave more encouragement,

telling me to call from Victoria Station in London. He'd persuaded me to wear a white shirt and tie to maintain appearances.
I neatly stuffed a joint inside my tie to help with the trauma of
landing in Luxembourg—alone.

CHAPTER 21

BOSTON CALLING, TWO YEARS LATER

I traveled through most of Europe and North Africa for 27 months. Within the first few weeks I met a Danish woman, Maria, while hitchhiking in Spain. She had an uncommon beauty about her that attracted me immediately. A potter, she was in Spain looking for creative ideas to expand her own work. We quickly became an item and went to Morocco together. As soon as I saw Tangier from the ferry, I told Maria, "This is what I've been looking for." Morocco was where magic could be found in abundance.

After a month in Tangier and Fez, she returned to Denmark and I joined her from London a few weeks later.

To my astonishment, Steve broke free from the ghetto and met up with us in Denmark in February 1969. That summer Maria, Steve, and I worked in Munich, saving for a trip across North Africa to see the Sahara in southern Morocco. What a trip it was, sharing Steve's triumphant return to the

Motherland. "For the first time, I'm in the majority, ya dig?" he told us. After losing our way in the mountains of Tunisia, we had only five days to hitchhike through Algeria. By issuing me a five-day transit visa, the Algerians were making a point of how they felt about the American government. After Algeria, we bypassed Casablanca in our haste to reach Marrakech, which was *the* destination in 1969. The Moroccan culture with its diverse music, elaborate architecture, and exotic dress was spellbinding. Of course the local marijuana, keef, was outta sight. But despite all the good times, the truth of the old saying, "three's a crowd," became obvious even to me. In the remote silence of the Sahara, Maria gave me an ultimatum, "Get married or get lost."

Married? I thought. *I'm just getting my groove together.* Why would I go to live in the boonies of Denmark where I couldn't speak the language and had little marketable skills to offer? We loved each other, but in no way was I ready for marriage.

Heartbroken, we said our goodbyes in Tangier in January 1971.

Steve and I went to London to find work. I landed a position at WHSmith, a bookseller in Sloane Square. Steve found a gig repairing clocks. We only went to hear jazz at the famous Ronnie Scott's a few times—a great club, but expensive. Meeting English women in London, or anybody for that matter, on our meager wages was near impossible. No surprise that Steve decided to return to Boston to pursue his career in electronics. I hated to see him go.

By July, I was alone in a dreary bedsit waiting for something to happen.

On a typical cold and dark December day, Laura, the cute Australian woman from the office at WHSmith, told me, "You have a long-distance telephone call from Boston."

Who could it be? I thought. *What's happened? People don't just call overseas for no reason.* Immediately my mind raced from one scenario to another:

The draft board wanted me.

My father or mother had died.

David had gone berserk during a drunken episode.

Picking up the receiver, my mind went blank.

"Gerard, it's Rodney." His voice sprung me back to life.

"Wow, glad to hear it's you. Ya know, getting overseas phone calls usually means bad news. So what's happenin'? Coming over?"

His pause gave me concern, or maybe it was just a bad connection. In a sober tone, he said, "I have news, something you should know."

Oh shit, there is bad news.

"Bobby died a week ago," I heard Rodney say in the same monotone.

Everything receded, the light grew dim, and his voice was barely audible. My knees buckled; I fell into a nearby chair, "What did you say?"

Rodney repeated what I desperately didn't want to hear, "I know it's hard to fathom, but Bobby's gone."

All I could say was, "Oh no, not Bobby!"

"It was hard to track you down. I saw Charlie, who…"

I wasn't listening. "Hold on, I need a second. What did you say?"

"Charlie—you don't know him—told me about Bobby, then I called your parents. Finding a phone number for WHSmith in Sloane Square took some effort."

"But what happened to Bobby?"

"It was an overdose."

"Ohhh, no! He seemed to be getting it together when I saw him just before I left. Maybe it was another act?"

"He *was* doing good. Then recently I ran into him on Boylston Street. He was high, but I didn't think it was scag."

Visions of Bobby lying dead with a needle in his arm made me nauseous.

"I knew you'd want to know before you came back. When *are* you coming back?" Rodney asked.

"I have no idea, not any time soon."

"I dig it. The place is just as fucked up, maybe worse. You ain't missing anything but Nixon on the news," Rodney said.

"I feel sick!"

"It's a goddamn shame, a waste. I miss Bobby too. Please take care of yourself."

"I wish I could talk. There is so much to say about Bobby, but I can't right now, " I managed to say.

"The time will come when you can fully express your grief," Rodney replied. "I know you loved the brother."

"I did, I really did. If I'd been more aware, with less fear, this might not…"

"Don't go there. It won't help." Rodney interrupted. "Bobby made his own choices. Both of us wish he could've accepted himself for the beautiful brother he was, but just like too many others in the same situation, Black or White, he ended up hating himself."

"You're right, but it's hard not to have regrets. I should let you go, this must be costing…"

"No, no, I owe it to both of you. And please take care of yourself."

"I did need to know, thanks for calling. So long."

"Later."

I went into the music-listening room to hide.

Frank, my coworker in the music department, noticed and asked what had happened.

"That's a real drag; I'm very sorry for your loss," he said. "Hold on. I'll be right back."

He returned with a slight grin, handing me a fat joint.

"Here man, go home. No one will notice. See you tomorrow."

Usually my bus ride upstairs on the #137 double decker bus to Clapham Common was enjoyable and relaxing. But not that day. All I could see was Bobby's face. All I could hear was his infectious laughter. The "what ifs" paralyzed my brain. If only he could have accepted his sexuality and hadn't resorted to heroin for relief.

Back in my gloomy bedsit, I tried to drown out the horror of losing my best friend by playing the old familiar jazz. But nearly every tune I played had some association with Bobby. I turned off the stereo.

I sat in silence for many nights, reflecting on Bobby's impact. First of all, he was the best friend I'd ever had. Then there was the music. He wasn't responsible for my initial interest in jazz, but he threw open the door to it. After we first met, Bobby was more than willing to discuss racial issues and African-American ghetto life while showing a genuine interest in what I thought. It was through Bobby that I made friends and became part of a shared experience. If given the chance, we could have moved beyond that dreadful bloody morning and resumed our deep connection.

Bobby showed me the world was more extensive and complex than I'd ever dreamt it could be. He liberated me from adolescent assumptions and set me on a course toward adulthood. There was so much left we could have explored and shared together. Now that opportunity had been snatched away. Yet even in death Bobby continued to teach, to expand my self-awareness, which now included mortality. No different than most young people, I'd assumed death was for others—that it didn't apply to me. Now his tragic end shattered that notion. The invincibility of youth couldn't save Bobby from the consequences of his actions. Nor would it save me from mine. Once I had assumed the possibilities in life were infinite, but now it was obvious that I wasn't as free as I'd previously thought. I asked myself, if each of us has an expiration date, what did I want before my life ran out? The world around me remained fascinating, but I realized that I'd been neglecting the inner quest, the realm which Bobby and I had explored through Coltrane's music.

With Bobby's passing, that search took on new importance and became my focus. But how to proceed was more daunting than boarding the Icelandic flight to Europe, alone, had been.

ACKNOWLEDGMENTS

I want to express my profound gratitude to everyone who saw me through this lengthy project.

To Christine Korfhage who convinced me the story was worth telling and became pivotal in moving the project forward.

To Bruno Debas for his insightful guidance throughout and for introducing me to the Hull Writing Group where Ricki Wilkes, Mary Ford, and Bruno showed infinite patience in reading my early drafts.

I thank Susan Dyment whose enthusiasm kept me motivated and also Bruce MacNelly, Frederic Duchamps, and Fletcher Lokey whose insights were essential.

How fortunate I was to find Jeff DiPerna, my editor, who went far beyond his job description and took a personal interest in my story.

I can't thank my wife, Roberta, enough for her unwavering support, expertise, and command of the English language where I was woefully lacking.

Nearly six decades have passed since I met Bobby. In spite of our all too short relationship, rarely does a day pass without acknowledging his profound influence. Robert E. Jackson, July 31, 1945 – December 5,1970.

ABOUT THE AUTHOR

Gerard Wiggins was born and raised in rural New Hampshire. He has lived in Boston with his English wife since the early 80s. A retired decorative artist in the interior design field, Gerard spends his time painting cityscapes, writing, and expanding his jazz collection. Since 2007, he and his wife have spent winters traveling in India. This is his first book.

www.gerardwiggins.com

Made in the USA
Middletown, DE
26 November 2023

43594719R00126